# your
## trajectory
## code

How to **CHANGE YOUR DECISIONS, ACTIONS,** and **DIRECTIONS,** to BECOME PART of the **TOP 1% HIGH ACHIEVERS**

# your trajectory code

## JEFFREY MAGEE

WILEY

Published by John Wiley & Sons, Inc., Hoboken, New Jersey
Published simultaneously in Canada

For general information about our other products and services, please contact our Customer Care Department within the United States at (800) 762-2974, outside the United States at (317) 572-3993 or fax (317) 572-4002.

Wiley publishes in a variety of print and electronic formats and by print-on-demand. Some material included with standard print versions of this book may not be included in e-books or in print-on-demand. If this book refers to media such as a CD or DVD that is not included in the version you purchased, you may download this material at http://booksupport.wiley.com. For more information about Wiley products, visit www.wiley.com.

Library of Congress Cataloging-in-Publication Data is on file.

978-1-119-04323-2 (hbk)

978-1-119-04333-1 (ePDF)

978-1-119-04332-4 (ePub)

10 9 8 7 6 5 4 3 2 1

# Contents

Introduction—Your Trajectory Code: The Mental DNA Imprint to Who You Are, What You Do, and How to Design an Adaptive Attitude for Achievement!                     1

**1**   Understanding Your Mental TC-DNA Imprint: How Your FIST Factor™ Influences the Lines You Follow                                                        11

**2**   Understanding How Your Identity-Purpose Statement™ Imprint and Trajectory Empower You to Manage Your Line                                            23

**3**   Walk the Line: Assuming Ownership and Trajectory Balance                                                                         37

**4**   Understanding Your X-Factor on Your Trajectory: What You're Best Suited to Do                                               47

**5**   Applying Your Player Capability Index™ to Your Trajectory Direction                                                                 57

**6**   Applying PFC FISHES to Your Life Trajectory for Balance and Inner Harmony                                                     79

**7**   Shift Happens...Trajectory Shift Drivers and Bridges That Create Sustained Positive Change                                      91

**8**   Understanding—and Fixing—the Gap between Lines for Trajectory Realignment                                              107

**9**   What Line Really Matters? Smart versus Safe Trajectory Decisions                                                             119

**10**  Intersecting Lines: Thinking about Lateral and Vertical Trajectories                                                           127

**11**  The Cracks in the Line: Relationships Can Make or Break Your Trajectories                                               135

**12** Alignment: Blending Trajectories with Others for
Shared Success 143

**13** The Power of Low Expectations 151

**14** Purposeful You and Your Trajectory Code:
Victim or Victor? Your Self-Talk Is Critical 157

**15** Conclusion: Trajectory Do-Over and Core Driver 163

About the Author 171
Index 175

# Introduction
# Your Trajectory Code

## *The Mental DNA Imprint to Who You Are, What You Do, and How to Design an Adaptive Attitude for Achievement!*

**The Trajectory Code™**

Watch Jeff live before you read this chapter online at www .TrajectoryCode.com.

## RE-DO YOU

Imagine being able to reboot your life, beginning at this very moment, given all you know and mentally possess. Imagine if you could bridge the gap from where you are in life to where you want to be, and then maintain that trajectory as you make greater gains, greater wins, and greater contributions to others.

The conscious and unconscious imprints upon your life from birth to the present date directly impact the trajectory that you take and the destinations you reach. Understanding your current, past, and future imprints allows you to manage your Line. This is how you'll get from where you are to where you want to be.

That is what this book will do. *Your Trajectory Code* is the universal truth for a better you. And if you understand what your Line is—where it is at all times, and the forces that influence it—you can do exactly that. Moving from good to great to significant requires that you understand and take ownership of your Trajectory Code (TC). These are the imprints we have unconsciously allowed to shape our psychology, and are therefore the behaviors that are consciously self-directed and accepted, and that guide our trajectory through life.

Nothing happens by accident. The impressions you carry, acknowledge, understand, and manage will influence your trajectory direction in the present, intermediate, and long term. Understanding these imprints and recognizing subsequent future conscious imprinting allows you to make a trajectory change at any time and attain even greater things—on both a personal level and on a professional level.

*Your Trajectory Code* will be the beginning of your journey, quest, and conversation along this pathway, but will by no means be the complete work you will undergo. The way in which you engineer your relationships, and experience the environments and culture for what you accept and internalize are all part of the process as well.

People in today's world are looking for new ways to achieve or deceive, to excel or derail, to grace or deface, to contribute meaningfully or make the case for ever-increasing entitlements. The question at either end of the pendulum is, what calibrates individuals and groups to have these polarizing mindsets and associated behaviors? It is the Trajectory Code™ that has wittingly or unwittingly been calibrated within each of us. We either expect that someone else will take care of things for us, or we recognize that we are responsible for our needs and goals. It is the latter group that sees the need to apply mental and physical labor into the equation.

There are countless examples within politics, labor, management, business, communities, families, personal relationships, religion, and even within our own internal dialogue over our imprinting. Often, our past experiences—whether personal or professional—influence our internal dialogue and cause us to believe that future interactions will be the same. A single negative interaction with a coworker, for instance, may lead us to assume that all future interactions will be just as negative—and we end up receiving exactly what we tolerate and condone.

Your Lines—the pathways of what you say, do, feel, and act—are represented by your motives, values, and psychological needs, each of which calibrate your trajectory on a daily basis. You design your own Trajectory Code to accept or reject any signal consistent or inconsistent with its architecture. In this way, you already possess everything you will ever need to attain greatness. *You* train your thoughts, cells, and behaviors to act and respond the way they do. Once trained, these elements want to maintain that trajectory. They remain open to anything consistent with that training and resist anything that challenges it or seems out of context. You can take ownership of your code and attain even deeper and more meaningful levels of greatness; or you can abdicate responsibility and allow others to determine your code and thus your destiny.

The Conference Board and *Harvard Business Review* reported in 2012 that research surveys show thousands of American workers had the lowest job satisfaction in 22 years. Research by Deloitte, HBR, and Gallup indicates that job satisfaction, individual happiness ratings, and increased quality of work is significantly linked to productivity and profitability. Some research even indicates as much as doubled profitability linkage to happiness factors. In fact, a 2012 *New York Times* article indicated that the cost of disengagement on America's productivity is more than $300 billion annually.

In 2012, Deloitte compiled a research white paper on technical professional skills and knowledge development. Seventy-two percent of Deloitte's top clients worldwide clearly indicated that this is the single greatest make-or-break point to business succession, while less than 7 percent believed their organizations weren't actually doing anything to secure their future and their success.

Even more alarming is that this level of disengagement occupied protestors' entitlement beliefs. And an individual's or an organization's Trajectory Code influences how we see ourselves and others. This perception—and the action that follows—leads to the achievement of immediate, intermediate, and long-term goals.

From 2000 through 2012, I served as the publisher for *PERFORMANCE/P360 Magazine* (www.ProfessionalPerformance Magazine.com). We showcased articles on achievement, success, and performance by the leading experts, celebrities, professional athletes, political leaders, best-selling self-help and business authors, original thought-leaders, entertainers, entrepreneurs, and business leaders from across the globe. We found a common thread to all editorial contributions and interviews—namely, that leaders are achievers and achievers have solutions. Losers make excuses, point fingers, lay blame, and deflect attention away from their inability to take responsibility.

So, how can you calibrate away from implosion destinations and make meaningful contributions and meaningful lives? It's as simple as A-B-C: The process by which you visualize your Trajectory Code (see Figure I.1).

1. Point A is always the Activating Event—the starting point that determines how your TC shapes your every action. From here, there are only two trajectories to track.

2. Point B represents the Line, where your actual behaviors, learned habits, personal standard operating procedures (SOPs), and emotional influences may direct your path. It is how you have trained yourself to think and act and typically represents your current reality—not your future goals.

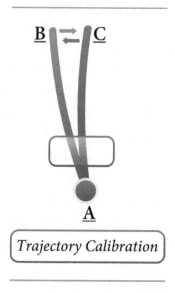

*Trajectory Calibration*

**FIGURE I.1    Your Trajectory Calibration**

**3.** Point C represents Consequence. Your Line is always the desired and intended consequence, the course to your intended goal, target, and trajectory for success. It is only by understanding the influences, alignments, and your Trajectory Code (the 1 percent factors, which we'll explain in greater detail later) that you attain Point C and ensure your Line is most efficiently executed. It is influenced and calibrated by your mission, vision, and values. Your Point C is calibrated and your momentum is maintained by very specific Key Performance Indicators (KPIs) that allow you to sequentially measure the immediate, intermediate, and long-term time spans as you progress forward to Point C.

A more profound question is whether the trajectory represented as Point B is taking you off track. If you were to extrapolate outward at the time of an action, could you recognize where it would take you in the end? Making trajectory recalibrations is exceedingly easy at the base line, represented by the circle at the base represented by Point A—as opposed to where most people wake up and recognize they are off trajectory!

Acknowledge, assume ownership, and rewrite (recalibrate) your Trajectory Code by focusing on the Line that matters. Remove or limit the influence of negative imprinting upon your Trajectory Code and ensure that your Trajectory Code is exercised (calibrated), to help you achieve your desired direction.

This book discusses in detail those factors that have influenced your trajectory thus far. We'll talk about how to harness those factors and leverage them for your advantage and for the future. We'll hone in on the influences to which you should willingly expose yourself for greater Trajectory Code enhancement.

Your trajectory calibration directly dictates your path. Understanding the marked space directly above Point A as those immediate actions after launching from Point A—and recognizing the examination of any action extrapolated into the future—will reveal whether you are heading towards Point B or Point C. This will then determine your ability to make a calculated adjustment, which is a mere 1 percent recalibration at that moment. These 1 percent recalibrations are typically easy to undertake, met with minimal internal or external resistance, and can yield significantly different outcomes.

Let's say you're trying to lose weight. Some examples of common 1 percent recalibrations are drinking water before you eat in order to eat less, or taking the stairs instead of taking an elevator. In terms of professional growth, small things like asking someone to review a critical e-mail before you send it would be a 1 percent recalibration.

Every decision and action you undertake impacts your trajectory and the Line you are on. Veering off course—even by the slightest degree—impedes your ability to arrive at your ultimate destination. Imagine a pilot attempting to circumnavigate the globe—if the pilot's trajectory is off by as little as one degree, he would not end up back at the same longitude where he started but would be off by more than 500 miles!

Most individuals and organizations miss these 1 percent opportunities and fail to realize that they are moving off their desired Line—until they awaken at Point B and see Point C off in the distance. They must then undertake a significant amount of work—often painful and wrought with resistance, blame, anger, and resentment—to get back onto trajectory track C. But even at this point, a true performer will accept the off-track trajectory and undergo the work necessary to reestablish themselves on the correct path. They do so by building a better *code*, eliminating the losers from their life, and drawing upon the champions. You can respond—which is an act of *logic* when you have the *facts*—and can take the appropriate action. However, you react—an act of *emotion*—when you engage in this process in reverse; that is, take action and then get the facts. This book will empower you to regain control of your trajectory and destiny, regardless of the situation or circumstances that you find yourself in.

At the end of each chapter, I have provided three simple questions for you to consider in reflection for that chapter and how to apply these ideas into your life for trajectory implementation and success.

# CHAPTER 1

# Understanding Your Mental TC-DNA Imprint

## *How Your FIST Factor™ Influences the Lines You Follow*

## SO WHERE DOES IT START?

Imagine you are in a time machine. The space your machine currently occupies is the present. Behind you is the past, and directly in front is the future. As you look outward, you see in front of you a massive windshield of life, representing the future opportunities, abundance mentality, possibilities, success, achievement, solutions, collaborations, partnerships, constructive imprints, and influences. Upward to the right of the windshield would be a small rearview-mirror representing your past—experiences, pity, blame, jealousy, revenge, cynicism, what was or could have been, challenges encountered, and negative imprints, influences, and people.

Most people's rearview-mirror images are overwhelmingly negative, and continuously stimulate a defeating internal conversation. Even more amazing is that the rearview mirror represents only about 3 percent of the windshield space—yet it's the area upon which most of us fixate!

Do you find yourself engaging in conversations of disparity or negativity as you view your past? Do you ever think about how that conversation just gains emotional momentum? Chances are that, during these times, you already have or are pushing away positive imprints—people, choices, opportunities, and so on. This is when the detrimental rearview-mirror talk consumes you. To make matters even worse, this is also a place where misery loves company—you typically attract others like you, until you have an army of bitterness. Now reflect on how this imprints your Trajectory Code. How has it influenced—and how will it continue to influence—your trajectory directions?

You may maintain your outside rearview mirror for perspective and benchmarking purposes. However, you must get a firm grasp on the negativity, rip it off and throw it away. Only when you are ready to live in the windshield of positive imprints will you be able to develop a more purposeful you.

One of my earliest code imprints that I carry consciously with me today—and one that had a large part in framing my windshield—was set into motion in a small rural farming community, where I was raised. My first-grade teacher, a woman named Ms. Murphy, calibrated my Trajectory Code for success by holding me back one year. I wasn't aware of it at the time, of course; I was very young, and mostly frustrated that it took me two years to get through first grade. Many years later, I recognized the powerful gift that Ms. Murphy and my parents gave me by holding me back. To be pushed forward when my brain was not ready would have damaged my TC for life. I would have been lost as my second-grade classmates easily grasped new education. Chances are, I would have acted out to deflect attention away from my frustration.

We all have stories and memories of early childhood, teenage years, and early adulthood. Everything that happened during that time is part of our imprinting. Some we had control over, and some was thrust upon us. Recognizing this allows us to control our trajectories and draw upon the imprints that serve us constructively. Manage these imprints and do not allow them to unwittingly dictate your future trajectory, learn how to also not become a victim to them or allow negative past imprints to become your excuse for not accelerating towards successful Point C attainment. This is how you enrich your TC with new imprints to further strengthen your aim and the Lines you follow.

These examples and stories may have activated your subconscious voices of emotions; so let's add to the dialogue and start to unlock these secrets to a TC that enables you to achieve the greatness within. The best place to start is by developing an understanding of how your own mental TC DNA imprint influences your Trajectory Code, and we do this by taking an inventory the early years. No matter our age, there are people that have had an influence on who we are and how we see ourselves. Some may still occupy conscious or even unconscious space in your mind. Some may still be alive and with you; others may have long since passed away, yet you can still see them and hear them in your mind.

If you recognize that there are such people in your head—and thus, your life—and you mentally bring them up on a sort of mental roster, some names may immediately come to mind. This may not be a long list if you really drill into this first examination or lesson. So take your right hand palm up and flex open your fingers. As you bring up the first and immediate names on this mental roster, assign one name per finger in a countdown.

I call this your FIST Factor™, or your mental board of directors. These are the people that have calibrated your Trajectory Code through life. By becoming aware of how these people have influenced your past and present, you can manage how much time you allow them to influence you in your future. Now you can recognize some of the imprinting from your past that in fact has played active or passive roles in guiding you to where you are today.

Spend some time really looking inward on how these people, places, events, and experiences have been there to shape who you are today within your FIST Factor™ (more detail on this concept in coming sections). If this is not the trajectory direction you seek, recognize that YOU and only you can rewrite the imprinting. By changing your FIST Factor™ and instantly altering your inner dialogue, you immediately adjust your Trajectory Code and thus trajectory direction in any situation. Simply acknowledge your initial FIST Factor™ and imprint forward from there.

Are these windshield or rearview-mirror people?

Here is another way to recognize how the mental imprint of these forces can subtly change within us—and thus potentially alter the Lines you plot and your trajectory destination without your consciously realizing it.

1. Imagine the grocery store you presently go to on a regular basis for your staples. Now as you look at your present FIST Factor

make-up, how many of the people you see have changed in the past year?

2. Now consider the grocery store you went to on a regular basis 10 years ago. Look at your FIST Factor make-up and see how many of them have changed in the past 10 years.

3. Consider that what you currently do professionally reflects on your FIST Factor make-up. Now go back 10 years: What were you doing professionally or where were you physically working nine-to-five? Do you notice any difference in names with a significant change in reference points?

4. This final reference will help you recognize how altering just one trajectory course variable can change the make-up of your TC and influencers, which can affect your entire trajectory calibration and destination in life. Where do you physically live today? Go back 10 years ago, today. Do you find any difference? If so, look at your FIST Factor. Any difference?

Notice with any of these questions that as you change a major life variable, you may have added healthier TC influencers. You also may have lost a great mental connection with which you should reconnect. Maybe you have already recognized some unhealthy influencers; try to replace or at least limit their TC influence time upon you. In this way, you can manage your Trajectory Code imprinting and take control of your destinations—by always being mindful of past imprint influences and future imprint needs.

Consider the example of 16-year-old 2012 Olympic gold medalist Gabby Douglas. Gabby's own mother realized that if she stayed in the East Coast inner city, Gabby's TC imprinting would have been stacked against any degree of life success in her discipline. So she sent Gabby to Iowa to train under a TC superstar and to live with an adoptive family. Both changes would most surely be constructive windshield TC trajectory direction calibrators—and subsequently success-oriented FIST Factor contributors.

Your TC starts with those people that occupy your mental space—the individuals that either consciously or unconsciously take up room in your head. Recognize who they are. Then, pull forward the ones that serve positive forward windshield time, limit the rearview-mirror voices, and add only focused achievers forward into your space.

You can have multiple FIST Factors. There might be one that serves as the dominant overall force for you. Or perhaps you have specific situational-driven FIST Factors made up of different people for different needs. Perhaps there is someone whose input you value in a work situation and from whom you seek guidance. That person's mentorship will accelerate your trajectory success at work. Imagine the level of trajectory direction achievement you could attain if you had access to a wide mental platform of superstars. This is the perfect reason to begin meeting and networking with a greater, richer, deeper circle of people today. One way to do so is to consider your FIST factors' FIST factors, as this will help to expand your network in concentric circles.

You can inventory your defeats and successes by recognizing how you internally process situations and events. We tend to invest more time on our defeats and allow our internal dialogue to replay the negative, instead of reflecting on a defeat simply as a lesson learned and an opportunity to avoid such a mistake in the future. Likewise, we spend far too little time reflecting on successes to learn from them. Imagine the trajectory success you could experience if you engaged in more internal constructive dialogues versus negative dialogues. The TC you carry has been shaped by the FIST Factor you carry, and there is a direct connection between your FIST Factors and your TC.

Now let's take your TC to another level by examining your trajectory direction calibrators. You can think of this as a sort of GPS that guides you and which you can continuously fine-tune for greater effectiveness. As we know, your FIST Factors serve as your internal guidance system and trajectory influencers. They open your eyes to windshield perspectives or hold you back through rearview-mirror doubts. Notice the percentage of time you spend, in any given hour, in positive or negative self-talk. Then multiply that for every 24 hours, and onward, for the amount of time in any given year of your life thus far. It can become very revealing and alarming for most to realize how much we've held ourselves back by listening to these limiting voices—voices that come more frequently from ourselves than from anyone else.

Consider a time when you found yourself in a perceived trauma or high-stress situation. Does a solution-oriented inner dialogue influence your trajectory response? Or is it an activated emotional reaction that kicks in and influences your inner dialogue? What does that inner conversation reveal in terms of quantity of viable solutions—or do you become even more panicked at an increasingly limited trajectory of options? When someone provides constructive feedback to you, do you in fact hear it as positive and make the changes they've suggested—or do you begin an internal debate or attack the messenger?

Just as the computer adage GIGO—garbage in, garbage out—claims, so too it is true for the TC that you design and reinforce. It takes conscious dedication to build a positive TC and to continue to hold yourself accountable to that TC.

Consider where you want your trajectory to take you, both in the present and in the long term. Think of a ladder leaning up against a wall to represent any endeavor you seek to aspire upward to. On the bottom rung of the ladder is always you, and anyone you seek advice, counsel, mentorship, or guidance from should always be on the rungs above you. Vet them from the perspective of what you already know to be true. If the people you surround yourself with can't push you up in any particular and specific need area, then you should not be allowing them or inviting them into your inner physical or mental circle.

One area of study I pursued in college was journalism. Our professors always were mindful to instill within us the idea that journalists report the news based upon fact, as arrived by other subject matter experts and verified by at least two additional unrelated sources. The Sunday paper and a portion of the evening newscast would be reserved for commentary provided by the elder, more learned journalist with perspective. Nowadays, we hear plenty of online and television reports based on hastily gotten and biased information. Without a balanced FIST Factor and inner dialogue, most people accept at face value what they hear and read, thereby arriving at uninformed viewpoints. Now imagine how this ignites your windshield or rearview-mirror energies and influences your trajectory. Thankfully, you can right your course to ensure maximum positive impact by recognizing how the people around you influence your Line's direction, length, richness, and distance.

To ensure the imprints and influences these FIST Factor calibrators have on your psychology are healthy, make sure you actually know the people that you seek counsel from before you allow them into your FIST Factor. There are five types of influencers to have within your FIST Factor, for balance. You can have more or less than five actual people as mental references, just ensure you have at least these five types of or categories of FIST Factor representation:

1. Family—A family member knows a side of you others may not, so have that side kept in check by selecting a valuable family member to serve
2. Friend—A friend knows a side of you others may not, so have that side kept in check by selecting a valuable friend to serve
3. Profession—A super achiever professional colleague anywhere in the world knows a side of you others may not, and understands your professional unlike a family or friend may understand, so have that side kept in check by selecting a valuable professional colleague to serve

4. Success—As you define it, the single most successful, accomplished person you know understands trajectories to achievement and Point B avoidance strategies unlike others, so have that side kept in check by selecting a valuable person to serve
5. Underdog—For lack of a different name, select someone you know that has and maybe does face adversity, challenges, roadblocks in life and illustrates how never giving up leads to accomplishment, and have this person in your head as a FIST Factor representative as well

If you allow influences inside your head that you do not actually know, then the imprint will be a phantom, unsubstantiated, rogue, nonvalidated influence. Although I believe that Oprah would be a great FIST Factor calibrator, I do not know her—so I do not have real-time mental videotape for calibration reference and I would be making decisions based on her as a phantom imprint. Knowing your FIST Factor individuals provides you with a more accurate and resalable inner dialogue about what they would or would not do in a trajectory situation in which you may find yourself.

Are you recognizing ways to Redo You yet?

Now think about what has influenced your FIST Factors—their respective FIST Factors—and how. How have they become who they have become, and how does that imprint upon you? This is another level of inner questions and answers you need to consider for a better understanding of their perspectives. Keep in mind that successful people want to associate with even more successful people. The company you keep tells a great deal about you.

---

### Redo You—The Line: Your Trajectory Code™
### Calibrators/Windshield Application Time

In order to plot your Line and ensure your trajectory growth and development, you as the reader must assume ownership of the calibrations that take place. You must address any issues that influence your personal trajectory growth, peer-to-peer interactions, or issues that hinder your Line, and assume ownership of your professional organizational trajectory advancement. Answer the following three questions to give you perspective on where you are on your Line.

1. **Personal (Positional) Growth:** Where are you now at Point A? Where are you on your Line based upon what you are doing? Is your trajectory headed toward Point B or Point C? What specific actions must you implement in the next 7/30/60 days to ensure your vocational positional trajectory pathway aims toward Point C?

_____

_____

2. **Peer-to-Peer Influence Accountability:** Where are you now? What is Point A? How are Lines intersecting based on what you are doing and how others are interacting with you? Is your trajectory headed toward Point B or Point C? What specific actions must you implement in the next 7/30/60 days with a Peer Accountability Partner to ensure your trajectory pathway aims toward Point C?

_____

_____

3. **Organizational Growth:** Where are you now? What is Point A? Based upon what you are doing, is your trajectory headed toward Point B or Point C? What specific actions must you implement in the next 7/30/60 days to ensure that your trajectory pathway within your organization moves you toward Point C?

_____

_____

*Trajectory Calibration*

# CHAPTER 2

# Understanding How Your Identity-Purpose Statement™ Imprint and Trajectory Empower You to Manage Your Line

Understanding the implications that your TC has upon your individual trajectory—both in your personal life and within a business context—are critical to arriving at your desired destination in a most efficient and expeditious manner. In the classic story *Alice in Wonderland*, Alice comes upon a fork in the road and she asks the wise yet challenging Cheshire Cat which way she should go. A defining moment occurs right then as the cat asks her, "Where do you want to go?"

Alice ponders and responds by saying, "I do not know."

"Then, it does not matter which way you go, does it?" the Cheshire Cat responds.

Far too many people and businesses operate that exact way every day. How can we make a decision on which way to turn if we don't know where we want to go? You must view every Point A as that fork—and you get to choose the Line that you will follow.

So let's further calibrate your ability to pivot from any Point A and ensure with greater clarity that your actions and those of the others around you continue down the trajectory of Point C destinations. Another significant influence upon the Line that you and others experience—and which will accelerate your success—has to do with your Identity-Purpose Statement.

Just as organizations have a mission statement that aims to guide its decisions and action, you as an individual should have a statement that serves as a benchmark for any endeavor you undertake and as a reference for any new deliverable. Though it's something that others have potentially helped you shape, it's your job to set out on it. Of course, you may have already realized that you're not seeking your own trajectory; rather, you're doing things to placate and accommodate others. This is why it is so necessary to develop an Identity-Purpose Statement to guide you along the way.

In our 2000 generational leadership book, *Coaching for Impact*, my co-author, Dr. Jay Kent-Ferraro, and I designed a communication engagement model built around the understanding of all invested parties and called it the Identity-Purpose (IP) Statement. Just as you have a personal Identity-Purpose Statement, so does everyone else. And once you understand both yours and others', you can forecast any future windshield or rearview-mirror behavior, response, or reaction. You have to engage others en route to your trajectory destinations—and understanding their Identity-Purpose Statements will ensure that you remain on course.

So let's explore what an Identity-Purpose Statement really is. The Identity part is your "what" factor—what you project to the outside universe, what you stand for, and what you will tolerate or not tolerate. It tells people what you value and what you do not value. Your Identity factor is the what or who you want others to see. The associated Purpose factor is what drives or motivates your Identity—the "why" behind the whats, or why that what is so important to you. In examining another person's Identity-Purpose Statement, it is important to understand their what, who, and why factors. That will provide you with a significant understanding to their trajectory choices in life.

An example IP Statement: I believe that every day I should contribute something meaningful and constructive to the people with whom I work. Your legacy is not in what you do, but in how you can accelerate others' trajectory success experiences at all times and in all ways.

The real power comes from merely understanding and acknowledging your Identity-Purpose Statement as it stands today, without judgment or overthinking. Now recognize that every decision you make tends to align with that Identity-Purpose Statement—as are the people we gravitate toward and associate with and the activities with which we involve ourselves. If your Identity-Purpose Statement is sound, so too will be your TC, and the subsequent influencers within it. If you do not like some of the things around you or people you tend to attract, examine your Identity-Purpose Statement. What could you change?

A-level people surround themselves with A-level people, whereas B-level people surround themselves with C-level people. It is one's Identity-Purpose Statement that drives these beliefs, actions, and subsequent FIST Factor. So are you associating with people that raise your performance bar? Or are you so insecure that you must be the smartest person in your mental and physical room?

Your Trajectory Direction is a result of a better understanding of your TC—tempered with a dose of reality. Successful organizations and people do what they are best at and let go of the rest. As such, this next TC idea may radically change how you see yourself and others. It may motivate you to reevaluate yourself on both a personal and professional level.

To gain clarity on how your Identity-Purpose Statement influences which Line you pursue, your ultimate trajectory or how your trajectory influences it, let's examine three clarity questions:

1. Examine the Trajectory Calibration diagram (Figure I.1) by using Point A for where you always are and Point C for your always-intended goals. Discern where you are headed based upon your decisions, actions, and the influencers around you. Are you headed toward Point B or are you in fact on course for Point C?

2. Are the members of your FIST Factor in fact serving you as shepherds, guardians, advocates, and mentors to shorten your learning curves? Avoid their mistakes, and accelerate your ability to have true gains and serve others in only the manner you can.

3. Recognize the generational, cultural, ethical, gender, ethnic, educational, religious, lifestyle, professional, social, and economic overlays that have and will influence your TC and which subsequently influence your Identity-Purpose Statement. *You* must decide what is right and wrong for you and live your own TC and trajectory calibration.

To design a balanced and healthy Identity-Purpose Statement, view your Identity-Purpose Statement as though it is an organizational mission statement. Only the vested core parties should serve as the essential stakeholders in designing or updating a mission statement, as it serves as the organization's TC against which all decisions should be benchmarked for execution. In the same way, your Identity-Purpose Statement serves as the calibrator for your TC.

You can start to build your Identity-Purpose Statement by answering six essential questions, the 5W and 1H letter model. Take a sheet of paper, write down these six words along one side, then write any words or sentences to illuminate each.

1. Who
2. What
3. When
4. Where
5. Why
6. How

**An example IP Statement:** I believe that every day I should contribute something meaningful and constructive to others I work with and serve. One's legacy is not in what one does, but in how one can accelerate others' trajectory success experiences at all times and in all ways.

It's pretty surprising how many people can't fluidly respond to "Who am I?" and "What do I stand for?"

Your Identity-Purpose Statement may have been imprinted early on by your environment, family, friends, school, community, and government—that is, every strengthening FIST Factor within you and more. But you can make conscious trajectory calibrations to alter your future trajectory to a more meaningful course.

Your Identity-Purpose Statement determines the Line you are on now. It keeps you open and welcoming to influencers consistent with your programming. If this is not the Line or Trajectory you desire, the solution is simple: Rewrite your IP and you can craft a different Line experience in life.

Recognize that your TC is comprised of the sum of who you are and what you have been subjected to (good and bad).

We often hear about people getting caught up in rhetoric about what TC changes they need to make without extrapolating that trajectory change to determine where that might take them tomorrow. People do a great job of directing everyone else's lives and dispensing advice without looking through their own windshield to recognize where they are going. Often, instead of just holding ourselves and others accountable, we allow people to deflect attention away from real TC Calibrators to lay blame upon others and become fixated upon TC Calibrators that really do not matter at the end of the day. Consider the examples of these that abound:

- A congressional leader discussing how the rich do not pay their fair share of taxes in America, while being one of the top 25 wealthiest members of Congress and refusing to write a check to the U.S. Treasury, despite saying that he feels the rich should be paying and despite that doing so himself would set a TC example.
- A state governor blatantly selling off a senatorial seat for favor and expecting to be exonerated.
- An entertainer lip-synching a song, forgetting her own words, and then expecting the audience to forgive her.
- Athletes taking drugs to enhance their performance, then blaming others when caught as justification for their behavior.
- Business people who cheat on their taxes or mistreat their employees and expect to be above question, because they are "leaders" in their community.
- It would be you and me . . . . And expecting others to … ?

Our TC either allows behavior to get us into trouble or keeps us calibrated for Point C destinations of achievement and success above reproach.

A clearly defined IP Statement will drive your inner passion, which fuels your commitment to freely assume ownership levels of the things, situations, and people you seek or that others expect. This is truly a secret that will excel you forward from those things that are congruent with your IP Statement.

A clearly defined IP Statement will drive your FIST Factor, to ensure your calibration is on track for Point C destinations. It will serve as a balance to inform and warn you when people are coming into your space that will propel you from your trajectory to Point C and align with them to attain their goals, thereby sending you off trajectory and toward Point B. A clearly defined IP Statement will assist you in vetting appropriate future FIST Factor candidates to align with, to serve, and be served by.

Consider the following six questions about your Identity-Purpose Statement—which should serve you as a mission statement serves a world-class organization:

1. Do you have one?
2. Have you been thinking about this? Should you start putting some ideas down now?
3. Where can you post your IP Statement so that you see it every morning when you wake as an immediate conscious calibrator?
4. Where could you post it for a mid-day reminder and check-up to ensure your trajectory is on course?
5. Where could you post it before going to bed, as one last conscious reminder of your life trajectory—so your subconscious can challenge the creative DNA you possess and the FIST Factor you have assembled to work on it while you sleep?
6. What FIST Factor or peer accountability partners can you share this with?

You must define your IP Statement from what you find meaning in. You will be able to use it to calibrate your actions and to guide the windshield conversations and actions versus rearview-mirror doubts.

Calibrating your IP Statement into the organizations to which your trajectories lead you—and ensuring that they all blend accordingly—is essential for all the parties involved to succeed. In working with organizations of excellence over the past few decades, it has become exceedingly clear that all of them have five interconnected mission statements (which as we've discussed, is essentially an IP Statement for the business world). One feeds the next and all have vested interest in one another. Everyone moves forward along their respective and mutual trajectory pathways. Of course, people will have differences of opinion. But if you can direct the conversation back to the mission statements when these differences come to light, it will be very easy to get back onto the trajectory pathway toward Point C—and to almost laughingly drop the trajectory pathway to Point B endeavors. The five interrelated mission statements are:

1. **The Organization Mission Statement** is at the top of the pyramid. It is designed only by the key stakeholders at the top and should give clear direction for everyone associated as to the 5W and 1H letter model discussed earlier, thus providing clear trajectory direction to all internal and external constituents involved. Your mission statement should always be able, in a complete sentence, to speak to the who, what, when, where, why, and how variables.

2. **The Team Mission Statement** (functioning work group, department, strategic business units, shifts, line work units, etc.) serves the organizational mission statement in part and should speak to the contributing piece it owns. Appropriate stakeholders design it as well. This becomes more micro to the macro language of the organization. This common

understanding then drives every trajectory undertaking and associations, alliances, affiliations, partnerships, new deliverables, and so on, to ensure support to the organizational mission statement and to ensure that there are no fiefdoms building.

3. **The Customer Mission Statement** should identify that you are there to serve. It is critical to understand the primary recipient of your work product, not the secondary or ancillary recipients. This common understanding then drives every trajectory undertaking and associations, alliances, affiliations, partnerships, new deliverables, and so on, at your team level. It allows you to keep a pulse on the market at the street level and to feed backward into your organization, ensuring that you always remain relevant.

4. **The Colleague Mission Statement** makes it clear that you and others have to have some degree of understanding of each others' roles. Knowing the other players on your team's Identity-Purpose Statement allows you to see their trajectory and understand why they either buy in or not to particular actions, activities, procedures, programs, and so on. This common understanding then drives every trajectory undertaking and associations, alliances, affiliations, partnerships, new deliverables, and so on, to ensure support to the organizational, team, and customer's mission statement and to ensure that there are no fiefdom buildings nor individual rogue trajectories or Point B destinations at the expense of yourself or others.

5. **The Personal Mission Statement** (Identity-Purpose Statement) is critical too. At this point, you can determine if you are a blend and match for the other four and how to calibrate your trajectories so everyone benefits. You may also come to the revelation that you are not willing or able to recalibrate your IP Statement and that the other four would be better served by your disengaging and going elsewhere in life.

You would never leave on a road trip to an unknown destination without directions or a map to guide your trajectory. Your IP Statement serves as your MAP—or Mental Action Plan. It must guide your every decision, action, alliance, collaboration, and partnership, and provide an accountability reference for what you should and should not do, no matter how inviting a situation or person may be. If it does not enable you to arrive at trajectory Point C more efficiently, then you should not engage in that trajectory activity.

As you reflect upon your trajectory thus far in life, you will likely recognize that a great calibrator of your endeavors have been the imprints upon your TC. Your IP Statement is what reinforces that TC and allows you to either be open, guarded, or closed to further imprints based upon their alignment to your TC. As you now move forward and determine the trajectory pathways toward your multiple Point C targets, YOU now must assume control of writing or rewriting your IP Statement and defining or recalibrating your TC to attain the meaningful life you are destined to live and share.

Consider the members of your FIST Factor, your interactions in the past 12 months with others, employment you had lost, people that you feel have wronged you, situations in which you feel you have not performed to expectations. Take some inventory of what has weighed you down mentally and recognize that they have had an imprint upon your TC and IP Statement. Realize that, beginning now, it is up to you to build what you really need into your IP Statement en route to your Point C destinations!

Remember—your conscious efforts in what you design as your IP Statement influences your TC. That in turn will guide both your conscious and subconscious brain and actions today and tomorrow. Individuals and organizations either have an implied IP Statement determined by their actions (or lack thereof) or a physically crafted and publicized IP Statement shaped by past, present, and future variables. This IP Statement influences which trajectory one believes they can attain. If you know your IP or another person's, you can now forecast their every action and trajectory pathways.

Author's note: Also, each of the PFC FISHES Model areas can serve to have multiple Point C targets as we will explain later in this book.

---

### Redo You—The Line: *Your Trajectory Code*™ Calibrators/Windshield Application Time:

In order to plot your Line and ensure your trajectory growth and development, you as the reader must assume ownership of the calibrations that take place. You must address any issues that influence your personal trajectory growth, peer-to-peer interactions, or hinder your Line, and assume ownership of your professional organizational trajectory advancement. Answer the following three questions to give you perspective on where you are on your Line.

**1.** Personal (Positional) Growth: Where are you now at Point A? Where are you on your Line based upon what you are doing? Is your trajectory headed toward Point B or Point C? What specific actions must you implement in the next 7/30/60 days to ensure your vocational positional trajectory pathway aims toward Point C?

_____

_____

_____

_____

**2.** Peer-to-Peer Influence Accountability: Where are you now? What is Point A? How are Lines intersecting based on what you are doing and how others are interacting with you? Is your trajectory headed toward Point B or Point C? What specific actions must you implement in the next 7/30/60 days with a Peer Accountability Partner to ensure your trajectory pathway aims toward Point C?

_____

_____

_____

_____

**3.** Organizational Growth: Where are you now? What is Point A? Based upon what you are doing, is your trajectory headed toward Point B or Point C? What specific actions must you implement in the next

7/30/60 days to ensure that your trajectory pathway within your organization moves you toward Point C needs?

_____
_____
_____
_____

Trajectory Calibration

# CHAPTER 3

# Walk the Line

## *Assuming Ownership and Trajectory Balance*

Winning organizations and individuals take ownership for everything that happens to them. They do not engage in the excuse game for not attaining performance expectations. You can begin to assume this kind of ownership in your own life—and create a climate whereby others assume ownership of their jobs, responsibilities, and the overall organization—by understanding how four factors are interlinked, and thus, where you must first direct your energies.

The burning question in most individuals' minds is, "How do we get *others* to assume a higher level of ownership?" With this question in mind, I began my homework assignment and learned the following:

- When you know the depth of your abilities (formal and informal education, technical and nontechnical training, certification and credentialed work, accolade experiences) and you draw upon and apply them appropriately, you succeed in accomplishment or a personal victory. When you experience a victory, your self-esteem goes up. The same then holds true in your engagement of others.
- When you are victorious, you become significantly more motivated to apply yourself, assume more responsibility, and actively participate. At this point the need to establish incentive and motivation programs becomes less necessary.
- When you're motivated by victories and successes, you become significantly more passionate about life and the endeavors you pursue.
- We then take ownership of those things and people we are passionate about.
- Ultimately, getting people to take more ownership starts by setting *them* up for victory.

I realized the power of this model, shown in Figure 3.1, by performing a reverse analysis of some of the most successful

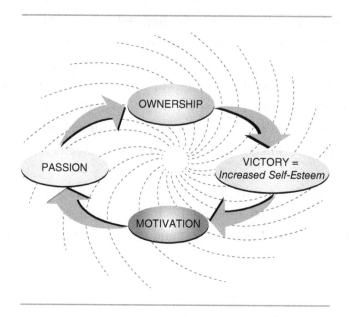

**FIGURE 3.1   The Ownership Model**

businesses today, many of whom have been my own clients. These include brands like Harley-Davidson, Army National Guard, Walmart, Boeing, Target, Anheuser-Busch, Vacuworx, SeaWorld, Southwest Airlines, Farm Credit Services of America, NASA, and many more. I found that performance execution is about accomplishing meaningful outcomes.

To do this, the starting point is not ownership issues at all, but rather setting yourself up for victories and success.

In order to move the Ownership Model—and therefore your trajectory—forward, the starting point is never ownership; it is always victory. This always puts performance in motion for execution and trajectory attainment. Ownership is the by-product of the previous three calibrators of trajectory success.

People who assume ownership seem to be among the most passionate about what they do, and are continuously motivated by what they do. This happens only when people are set up for victories, by doing those things that they are best mentally and physically equipped to undertake. All of this, in turn, feeds one's self-esteem. And when you operate from a level of high self-esteem, it is both exciting to see what you can accomplish and revealing to see what prompts you to then assume more ownership.

For you to attain greater and sustained levels of success, you first must shed some mental childhood DNA. For example, think about how many times you have heard or told someone:

- *Identify what you are good at in life and always be looking for opportunities for yourself.* Heard that line before? If so, continue with that level of operation—this breeds success. Often, the people who surrounded us growing up—parents, teachers, coaches, and so on—would make this comment in reference to awards we might receive. These are areas where greater success can be leveraged and where we should direct our actions for increased trajectory success. Perhaps it was academics, or sports, or art, or even just relationships. You know where you excel because you feel comfortable—and because people point it out to you! Keep your focus in this area, whatever it is in your adult life.
- *Identify what you are good at and recognize what you are weak at. Then when you find yourself having to do something that is not your strength, you can draw upon some of your strengths to complement your weaknesses and most likely prevail and be successful.* Heard that line before? If so, continue with that level of operation—this breeds success. The idea here is to actually limit your time working in, or being expected to work in this space. Delegate opportunities to others in areas where they excel and where you might not, so that you can concentrate your efforts on doing what you're great at. So maybe you're fantastic at giving presentations, but not so hot with the preparation required beforehand. Have someone help you get all your ducks in a row before you speak to a big audience, so you can feel confident in your delivery.

- *Identify what your core or net weaknesses are and then apply yourself and work to overcome them.* Heard that line before? If so, do *not* continue with that level of operation. True success in business by organizations and individuals means that they do not invest time, money, or energy here. So too should be your trajectory expectation.

Consider what it does to a person when he or she experiences a lack of victories. Then ask what that does to their passion. It becomes very clear why people won't want to assume more ownership of the situations, activities, projects, or jobs that continue to set them up to either be an active participant in the problem, or an active participant in the solution.

Why do some individuals shy away from taking control of a task and executing it to a high level of performance success? There are usually four factors at play here:

1. We tend not to volunteer or sign up for endeavors that do not play to our abilities or passion. This drives us toward non-victories, which in turn, drives our self-esteem downward. Who wants to keep doing something that is embarrassing or makes them look stupid in the eyes of their peers?
2. We find that with lackluster victories we spend a disproportionate amount of time trying to motivate others or ourselves in an attempt to do the things that do not inwardly and innately excite us anyway. Why? Because we do not play to what we are good at in the first place. (We'll elaborate on this in the next two chapters.)
3. Then, because we are not excited about what we are doing or those with whom we are associating, we have to fake the feeding of our passion. We engage in ceremonial activities, events, and celebrations to force-feed our appearance of being passionate.
4. This, in turn, manifests as an individual's lack of stepping up to an opportunity and assuming ownership. Then we are left

with abdication, excuses, procrastination, and people seemingly being oblivious to needs and situations.

While working as Boeing's longest-invited leadership consultant and performance speaker, I strategized with their global human capital development leaders while simultaneously working with Anheuser-Busch's leadership development team. It became clear that in order to create ownership DNA with the new professionals that they added to their teams, it was vital to position people for victories, and to create systems and environments that supported this endeavor.

You can see this concept play out with positive, or far too often, negative results, as you look at major businesses. Systems have matured that allow individuals with success and victories to ascend upward into positions that they can truly screw up. In most cases, these are good people that mean well, but they are placed into positions and expected to assume ownership, even though they lack the competency to execute their roles as true performers. This is additionally adversely impacted by their vanity, which precludes them from asking for help.

When famed CEO Jack Welch retired from GE, there was a stable of next wave executives for the GE Board to select from. When Jeff Immelt was selected as successor, many others subsequently left GE to become CEOs to other leading businesses. Within a few years several of these CEOs were unable to lead those new companies to success and were let go. None were truly *ready* to be leaders, as their trajectories indicated; they simply wanted the designated title.

This model holds true whether talking about the C-suite or the frontline sales of an organization—whether engaging professionals within the Centurion or baby boomer generation, or the younger entry-level side: Generation X, Generation Y, or the Millennial generation. (Chapter 8 will go into more detail on performance execution application with differing generational segments.)

Wouldn't you think there has to be a way to transition yourself and others away from disappointment and toward success? There are six specific ways every successful person and organization must go about creating a universe in which you and others assume ownership of your positions in life and become victors instead of victims.

Some organizations engineer a culture of one-team, one-organization, and thus, one-success. Southwest Airlines posted 90 consecutive quarters of profitability at a time when practically all other airlines sustained continued deficit operations, bankruptcy management, and a cutback mentality. How, you may ask, could Southwest Airlines do this? Simple! They instill into every employee and team member at every level that if consumers don't choose their organization, they do not make money. If they do not make money, no one wins in the end. While most major legacy airlines boast jet turnaround times of 45 to 60 minutes with between eight and 12 ramp professionals, Southwest can turn a jet in 13 to 30 minutes with just three professionals. That is how great their motivation is.

Everyone at Southwest understands that when a jet is on the ground, the team loses money. As a result, everyone has a sense of urgency to assist in any way possible and ensure that the jet is turned expeditiously. That is a team that assumes ownership in multiple ways to ensure performance execution.

Here are two critical observations of true trajectory success, on both an individual basis and an organizational level:

1. There never is a lack of people that are envious of others' accomplishments. That line seems endless.
2. I have never seen a line of people who envy the work it took to generate those accomplishments—have you?

Individuals who experience more trajectory direction successes and achievements than others place themselves in positions of greater quantitative victories and surround themselves with—associate, align, hire, volunteer, and so on—individuals that reinforce the healthy FIST Factor. They engage in inner and outward dialogues geared toward greater accomplishments. And when they face challenges, they're more equipped to calmly work through challenging situations for healthier outcomes.

When you do experience victory, it's critical to take a moment to mentally celebrate and reflect in that success. We need to feed our psychology with accomplishment, and see results of efforts we engage in and the output of our labor (whether mental or physical). With this celebration (inward or outward, private or public) we recycle our IP Statement and reinforce our TC to eagerly embrace the next opportunity to engage and showcase our Player Capability Index (PCI) toward another victory, it becomes addictive.

Surround yourself with individuals that will guide your trajectory toward Point C destinations and hold you objectively to who you are and a reality base line. It serves no purpose to lie to yourself or others at this stage in your TC building or rebuilding efforts.

---

**Redo You—The Line: *Your Trajectory Code*™**
**Calibrators/Windshield Application Time:**

In order to manage your Line and ensure your trajectory growth and development, you as the reader must assume ownership of the calibrations that take place. You must address any issues that influence your personal trajectory growth, peer-to-peer interactions, or hinder your Line, and assume ownership of your professional organizational trajectory advancement. Answer the following three questions to give you perspective on where you are on your Line.

**1.** Personal (Positional) Growth: Where are you now at Point A? Where are you on your Line based upon what you are doing? Is your trajectory headed toward Point B or Point C? What specific actions must

*(continued)*

*(continued)*

you implement in the next 7/30/60 days to ensure your vocational positional trajectory pathway aims toward Point C?

_____

_____

_____

_____

2. Peer-to-Peer Influence Accountability: Where are you now? What is Point A? How are Lines intersecting based upon what you are doing and how others are interacting with you? Is your trajectory headed toward Point B or Point C? What specific actions must you implement in the next 7/30/60 days with a Peer Accountability Partner to ensure your trajectory pathway aims toward Point C?

_____

_____

_____

_____

3. Organizational Growth: Where are you now? What is Point A? Based upon what you are doing, is your trajectory headed toward Point B or Point C? What specific actions must you implement in the next 7/30/60 days to ensure that your trajectory pathway within your organization moves you toward Point C needs?

_____

_____

_____

_____

*Trajectory Calibration*

# CHAPTER 4

# Understanding Your X-Factor on Your Trajectory

## *What You're Best Suited to Do*

To live a more purposeful life, you must engage in victory analysis by developing a tough-love understanding of what your X-Factor™ is and what it reveals about individuals, teams, departments, business organizations, and any other enterprise. This serves as the core driver to everything you should do as well as what you need to let go of. Once you have a firm grasp on the X-Factor concept, you'll have a much easier time shaping your future TC imprints, your FIST Factor, and evaluating your own Identity-Purpose Statement to make any necessary adjustments.

So let's explore this next idea. The "X" in X-Factor represents an endeavor and is in essence anything that you would like to track. Let "X" represent the word success. Now mentally frame the word by how you would define that word. No matter what you say, you are correct. Some examples are:

- Happiness
- Peace
- Respect of others
- Integrity
- Material possessions
- Career
- Family
- Community standing or involvement
- Finances
- Inspirational drivers
- Social standing or involvement
- Health
- Education
- Spirituality

By applying this concept, you will see how to set yourself and others up for performance execution success and work through meaningful trajectory direction. Ideally, you should have designed—or will design—your Trajectory Code to lead to your windshield success or rearview-mirror disappointments. Understanding and applying the X-Factor is about how you can avoid the suc-factor in life. Recognize that this is "suc" and not "suck."

Let's use athletics to represent the X-Factor. If we were to look at any high school campus on any given day:

- What percentage of the students would be good enough to make it into any varsity sporting team? What number comes to your mind? There is no statistical data to confirm this model; so just use your gut and common sense to drive your answers.
- What did you say? One, 5, 10, maybe 20 percent would be good enough to make the varsity team?

Now, out of 100 percent of the estimated 1.1 million varsity high school athletes (NCAA/CBS Sports Digest data, 2008–2009) on high school campuses, on any given school day:

- What percentage would be good enough to earn a scholarship and play at the collegiate level? Again, there is no wrong answer, and there is no statistical data to confirm this model. Just use your gut and common sense to drive your answers.
- What did you say? Less than 1, 5, or maybe 10 percent would be good enough to make the collegiate varsity team level?

Notice that as we track the X-Factor, the more proficient we expect someone to be, the smaller that population pool becomes. Finally, out of 100 percent of the estimated 28,800 collegiate varsity athletes:

- How many would be good enough to move onward and play that sport (their X-Factor) at the professional level?
- Less than 3, 2, or 1 percent would be good enough to make the professional level, right?

The point is, as you look at yourself and what you do, you are the professional. Whatever the percentage you said from above, represents you; not everyone can do what you can do!

So what would lead you to believe that you can be a pro at everything? Better yet, why should the people we sometimes elevate with expectations of greatness be able to perform in every position or situation we place them into as a professional? These are unrealistic expectations.

Make sure that you reflect upon the life-changing and life-impacting revelation of the X-Factor model (see Figure 4.1).

From the previous questions, you and I could, at best, be a success (circled in Figure 4.1) 20 percent of the time. The other 80 percent of the time—well, notice what has a box around it in the X-Factor.

Again, using the earlier questions as a reference to better understand the X-Factor concept, 80 percent of the time one would suc. Now you can see the difference between setting yourself or someone else up for success versus suc.

High-performance stars and those who understand performance execution limit their exposure to those things that they know—the things they suc at and increase their exposure to opportunities to excel at what they know they are successful doing. Focusing upon your success factor and ensuring your TC reinforces this; it will allow you to achieve even greater gains faster. By continuously recognizing that your trajectory pathway

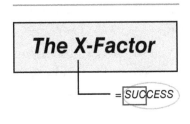

**FIGURE 4.1   The X-Factor Model**

is either heading to Point B or Point C, you're able to make 1 percent recalibrations.

Need an example? Let's consider Louis Gerstner—the only person to serve as CEO of three different Fortune 500 firms—American Express, RJR Nabisco, and IBM—each of which was on the brink of bankruptcy when he arrived, and all of which were highly profitable upon his departure.

Most likely, Gerstner's arrival at American Express went something like this: He came in, sat down, and assessed his executive team. They looked right back at him, perhaps expecting that Gerstner had some magical X-Factor that would turn the firm around and aim it toward profitability once again. Instead, he opened a discussion with the team, having each person explain the road to success as they saw it. This conversation gave team members the opportunity to share their own X-Factors. When the conversation came full circle, he stood, and announced that they all had the right answers, and his job was to support them while they executed their game plans. As he left, they gave him a standing ovation. He learned at that moment that whenever you are in the suc zone, someone around you will be in the success zone. You merely need to let them shine.

Gerstner recognized his own X-Factor and he drew upon others' to attain a new level of success. Once you apply this formula, it will change how you see yourself and others. More often than not, the kind of tough love this concept unearths is something most people are reluctant to apply. There are countless individuals who would prefer to continue their "oh, pity me" victim status.

Don't be one of these people. Look deeply into the mirror of life, pronounce what you suc at, and stop doing it. Do not allow past circumstances or a desire to appease others drive your movement. Identify what you are destined to be a success at, and live in the windshield!

As I detailed in my previous book, it is critical to realize that performance execution comes from having as many people as possible positioned in their respective X-Factor zones—and then getting out of their way. When you are in your suc zone, there is a great likelihood that someone around you is in that same zone. And while you may suc at something, someone else is successful at it. Have that person rise to the level of opportunity to assume ownership and lead others (and that can mean you) to performance execution greatness.

When you play with your X-Factor's potential, you push your TC forward. It affects every decision you make, and thus, influences the trajectory of your life.

We can observe some industries, professions, and individuals that really grasp this concept—people and organizations that truly live and die by continual real-time assessment designed to ensure that they both live their X-Factor and welcome continuous feedback by any means possible. And we generally don't find these examples in the mainstream business world or government agencies, but rather in the world of professional athletics.

Notice the TC and FIST Factor influencers. If you were a professional athlete, would you:

- Have someone tape your practices and game performances for analysis immediately afterward, in hopes of improving?
- Review a tape of your competitor's performance for analysis, in hopes of attaining more performance juice and success?
- Review the tape(s) of the best athletes in your industry to benchmark your performance in hopes of attaining more performance juice and success?

This example makes it clear that trajectory success and Point C experiences happen by design and not by accident.

Of course, most athletes would answer YES to all of these, which explains precisely why an athlete is either in their X-Factor zone and successful, or loses their juice very quickly. Only the best of the best survive. They do so by first playing to their

X-Factor; second, by continuously seeking out performance feedback; and third, by working to refine and improve their skill set. That calibrates your TC for peak performance and not mediocrity.

By now, you recognize how your TC has been shaped and still influences you in your professional life, and are beginning to gather some feedback in that vein. Most of us only receive professional feedback once or twice a year in the form of a performance evaluation, which is often heavily tied to performance pay and promotion. We do not invite this feedback as an athlete would—that is, 24/7 for the sole purpose of merely becoming the best we can. This is a distinct difference in our TC calibration.

When asked about his first race defeat in the 2012 London Olympics by pool-side commentators, renowned swimmer Michael Phelps immediately went into windshield language— that is, he indicated his focus was not on what he did not do, but on what he needed to do next. Imagine that organizations operated this way, instead of using mathematically driven, one-size-fits-all performance review systems that are facilitated far too infrequently to have relevant applications. And what makes it even more challenging for people to identify, develop, and attain their X factor is that many become defensive when receiving performance feedback, instead of accepting it for what it is and acting upon it openly.

Many people receive imprints early on that give them the idea that they are supposed to do something specific with their lives. Of course, these are usually prescribed by someone else and not calibrated to what individuals personally desire. As a result, many people lead a life of desperation and wandering Point B trajectories. This can get further complicated if those calibration influences are members of their FIST Factor and dominate their inner dialogues. This can cause a person to have continued mid-level victories, hovering somewhere between suc and success their entire life. The conscious and unconscious imprints upon your life—from birth to the present date—directly influence the trajectory you take and the destinations you reach.

To break out of this cycle, you must be able to clearly identify what you excel at and how to scientifically improve that quotient for greater trajectory success and ways to leave profound legacy imprints upon others. The only thing scarier than an incompetent person is one who wears a self-absorbed mask of competence when everyone around them sees the reality!

---

### Redo You—The Line: *Your Trajectory Code*™ Calibrators/Windshield Application Time:

In order to manage your Line and ensure your trajectory growth and development, you as the reader must assume ownership of the calibrations that take place. You must address any issues that influence your personal trajectory growth, peer-to-peer interactions, or hinder your Line, and assume ownership of your professional organizational trajectory advancement. Answer the following three questions to give you perspective on where you are on your Line.

1. Personal (Positional) Growth: Where are you now at Point A? Where are you on your Line based upon what you are doing? Is your trajectory headed toward Point B or Point C? What specific actions must you implement in the next 7/30/60 days to ensure your vocational positional trajectory pathway aims toward Point C?

   _____

   _____

   _____

   _____

2. Peer-to-Peer Influence Accountability: Where are you now? What is Point A? How are Lines intersecting based upon what you are doing and how others are interacting with you? Is your trajectory headed toward Point B or Point C? What specific actions must you

*(continued)*

*(continued)*

implement in the next 7/30/60 days with a Peer Accountability Partner to ensure your trajectory pathway aims toward Point C?

_____

_____

_____

_____

3. Organizational Growth: Where are you now? What is Point A? Based on what you are doing, is your trajectory headed toward Point B or Point C? What specific actions must you implement in the next 7/30/60 days to ensure that your trajectory pathway within your organization moves you toward Point C needs?

_____

_____

_____

_____

*Trajectory Calibration*

# CHAPTER 5

# Applying Your Player Capability Index™ to Your Trajectory Direction

Here it is, understanding the DNA blueprint ot your Trajectory Code is held within the understanding of this formula. This is the game changer to success.

This chapter will explore how to truly identify your X-Factor and measure your incremental trajectory steps to greatness. Imagine one of your FIST Factor calibrators were a world-class human capital coach. You'd then be able to see the objective talent management and thorough analysis of your competencies through the understanding and dogged utilization of the Player Capability Index™ (PCI). This reveals what your X-Factor may be, where you can grow it further, and most importantly what it is not.

This next commonality will radically change your internal and external conversations, as well as your trajectory in both your personal and professional life. It will change how you see yourself and others, and influence how organizational systems are run and how they hire, promote, and give employees further opportunities.

This next fundamental commonality is an objective diagnostic tool that will impact your performance quotient, trajectories, and your ultimate Line. The Player Capability Index calls your bluff on unrealistic inner windshield dialogue by giving you a pathway out of self-defeating rearview-mirror conversations. It also provides you with a scientific accountability formula, to replace FIST Factor calibrators (individuals) in your psychology with what you truly need to excel.

Let's go back to the time travel you experienced in Chapter 3. Your mind either focuses forward through the windshield of life—your future performance execution and success—or it keeps flashing into the rearview mirror, providing excuses for the things you never attained and explanations for why you are not progressing. Now you can see specifically where you need to concentrate dedicated efforts to possess the abilities to propel along the trajectory pathway you are meant to experience.

Corporate think-tank The Conference Board recently conducted a survey of hundreds of top businesses and thousands of corporate professionals and found that:

- Fifty-six percent of survey respondents indicated that they are disengaged in the workplace.
- Seventeen percent of survey respondents indicated that they are actively disengaged in the workplace.
- Thus, 73 percent of workers are not in their X-Factor and are looking for ways to provide minimal effort for maximum payment. Even worse, many times these people are not set up for success by those who have influence and are charged with the development of employees as organizational assets.

Imagine the level of inner negative dialogue these individuals must experience. Imagine what their FIST Factor must look like. And imagine the blurred IP Statements they must possess.

Next, imagine the effectiveness and performance execution you could experience if these players with these attitudes had their futures freed up, so that someone with integrity, drive, and self-worth could have their job opportunities.

Recently, the American Institute of Certified Public Accountants (AICPA) and the CEOs of the largest 100 CPA firms in America engaged in a real-time electronic survey on the issues of human capital performance and the competency capital within their respective organizations. Three major points became very evident:

1. Most (not all) have a human capital strategic plan for developing their employees, cultivating their future talent management needs, and establishing a succession plan. Do you?
2. Amazingly, however, the majority never referenced the document(s) or plan in the previous 12-month cycle as a tool to gauge their policies, guide their actions, or drive their internal development procedures. Do you?

3. When a partner or key human capital player leaves their team, the majority begins the succession development and transition of responsibilities as a real-time endeavor in the subsequent 6 to 12 months. What do you do?

To put this into your trajectory calibration language, we are talking about your Identity-Purpose Statement. As a performance coach to coaches, educators, and professionals alike, what alarms me the most is that people and organizations no longer see individual human capital development as a paramount need. This trend has dramatically altered the possible trajectory outcomes for both organizations and individuals. It therefore becomes even more so your responsibility to assume ownership of your trajectory and begin building a better and more dependable you.

Many times people wonder why leaders, colleagues, politicians, friends, or even family members around them seem to be people who should excel, yet flounder instead. If you really want an answer to these questions, check their FIST Factors that influence their self-expectations and inner dialogue to their beliefs, then apply this diagnostic formula below that I call the Player Capability Index model on them for a better clue. We frequently forget to ask about other people's X-Factor as much as we ignore our own. We're more apt to respond to our emotions and what is popular, than to what is sound, logical, and right to guide our actions, decisions, and encouragement of ourselves and others.

You can hold yourself accountable to continuous trajectory development by deploying something I call the Player Capability Index (PCI) model on yourself to ensure you know what your real human capital X-Factor is. Then apply it to others, so you can attain greater performance execution outcomes from them as well.

The following formula shows us that it truly is a combination of your IQ (Intelligence Quotient), and your EQ (Emotional Quotient) that drives your performance execution quotient toward your ultimate trajectory direction.

When I coach an individual—or even when I look inward at myself, my FIST Factor, and the core capabilities I have to attain the trajectory excellence—I use this model to guide my inner dialogue and outward efforts. Consider this diagnostic formula, whether reduced to a computerized Excel spreadsheet, built into online or hard-copy employment applications, or used as a self-assessment.

This formula can be self-applied or externally applied in objectively analyzing another person. Ask yourself how each letter in the formula pertains to you—and more importantly, to what depth you can answer each letter, as it relates to you:

$$C = (T2 + A + P + E + C)E2 \times R2 = R$$

1. R (starting on the far right side of the formula) stands for the Results you would like to generate. Results by other names would be the output, final work product, outcome, job position statement/description, requested task, customer request, goal, trajectory target point desired or expected. To get the R, you must know who you are (or who the other person is) in terms of what your core capabilities (far left side of the formula) really are.

2. C = Capability. You derive this from a combination of each letter within the parenthesis in the formula reading left to right. In essence, the letters inside the parenthesis represent your mental DNA and serve as the baseline to your trajectory thus far in life, which is drawn upon appropriately and continuously enriched as you evolve daily throughout your life.

   By understanding the legitimate true C within this model, you can grow and hold yourself and others accountable fairly and even with tough love. You now make logic-based, sound, and nonemotional popular choices. Remember— successful people (leaders) make smart decisions, not safe decisions!

**3.** T = Training, which includes any and all forms of education that you can acquire—formal or informal, technical or nontechnical, certification or noncertification driven. Any deliverable or distribution channel (i.e., traditional classroom or virtual, printed books, electronic books/texts, interactive texts, self-study, social mediums, magazines/journals, DVD, podcasts, YouTube, webcasts, webinars, teleseminars, online search engines, Skype, other/evolving electronic mediums) is included in this area.

There are two interpretations of the T. The first takes place in the present tense—the things that represent your current knowledge set. It encompasses any relevant deliverable or distribution channel from birth to the present date. A need for a comprehensive archive of the knowledge you or someone possesses is necessary to understand the value you can bring to others. Most individuals' and organizations' trajectories have been grossly miscalibrated to understand what T is actually drawn upon for any given work product. Specifically, we have been conditioned to value formal education and devalue informal education. Imagine when any traditional employment job application process gets to the T section; it asks for a person to chronicle the highest level of education (T) attained—where, when, and in what areas. It seldom continues by asking a person to detail the last 50 self-study, seminars, or online courses the person has participated in or graduated from.

Now if you've learned from all of this self-reflection that you lack the T necessary to have the C, you could make this letter T2. The second T represents the further or future training development and acquisition one needs. Once you apply T2, it guides the specific Technical skill sets and Professional skill sets needed to perform. This area alone is infinite and must be never-ending to remain relevant and cutting-edge. You can acquire this T via traditional channels through books, instruction, and face-to-face classroom settings, as well as evolving through traditional channels online, self-study, and so on.

Recognize as well that the pathway to effective knowledge acquisition for yourself always involves a psychological and chronological sequence to learning. Ensure that you flow forward systematically, so your brain absorbs and builds off of each essential knowledge point and learning endeavor.

4. A stands for Attitude, which is something we project in many ways. This is your desire, willingness, self-initiative, and self-confidence. We convey attitude by the way we act, talk, dress, and engage others. It is designed and supported by a healthy and diverse balanced FIST Factor, which drives your Performance Quotient (PQ) as drawn from the depth of your IQ and EQ and which will directly determine your trajectory pathways.

5. P is for Performance. This reinforces whether you know how to do something or not and shapes your overall capability levels. True X-Factor professionals seek continuous constructive feedback to always improve their abilities and standards of performance execution excellence. It also allows them to benchmark their efforts against other industry leaders. Understanding what you excel at and what you can merely perform to an acceptable standard is critical at this point. A great athlete, entertainer, celebrity, entrepreneur does not do that which they are seen as mediocre at doing!

Freely asking for critical behavior based feedback is essential. Looking at a specific task you are undertaking and asking whoever assigned it to you—or the person to whom you're delivering it—for a comprehensive relevant matrix to measure your performance, along your trajectory, to ensure you are both on track and excelling is also essential. This allows you to continuously raise the performance bar and recalibrate the matrix as appropriate for even greater effectiveness. Having a matrix designed to help you improve performance—one that is unrelated to pay/compensation increases or promotion/job advancement—is most critical for true TC and FIST Factor enrichment and ultimate buy-in as it relates to one's Identity-Purpose Statements.

Let's say that someone provided critical or affirmative feedback in the form of praise when you had accomplished something. The typical "You did a great job" is really too vague when laid against this formula. So the next time you are receiving a performance review, ask for specifics that will help you determine precisely what behavior to replicate. Imagine your manager says you're a great listener. Solicit behavior-specific comments to what your manager saw you do that she liked. Perhaps you were patient, made eye contact, took detailed notes, did not interrupt, or acknowledged the other person's comments as they made them. Now you have specific future actions to make your performance trajectory.

6. E = Experiences—both those that enhance and hinder your capabilities. Think of all the people, places, and things that you have come into contact with, that have consciously or sub-consciously influenced who you are. This will give you critical insight into how you may or may not perform. Constructive, positive, nurturing experiences shape your performance in one direction and determine your outlook. Conversely, the trauma you have endured also plays on your psychology. These same types of forces can be deployed in your future, to either further reinforce how you have been influenced or how you may have been influenced differently.

   This is critical to TC development and the cultivation of your overall capabilities, to recognize the people, places, things, tasks and job assignments, geographic imprints, and so forth, that can further shape and reinforce one's current and future trajectories. To know this about yourself—and to learn these trajectory imprints that others possess—can allow you to draw upon them smartly or compensate for what others have or do not have.

7. C = Culture, of both your personal and professional life. We can define our culture at a macro level and gain a greater understanding by digging into any individual cultural variable at micro levels such as your ethnicity, gender, generation, geographical region (continent, nation, state, county, city), organization (company, business, industry, division, team, work unit), socioeconomic status, life-style, profession/trade, religion, family, ancestry, and so on. It is endless and shapes the overall you and your trajectory in life. All of this combines to determine your net human capital DNA, and is something you influence on a regular basis.

   Culture shapes your trajectory in respect to the places you have lived in, worked in, and associated with. The individuals and related privileges that may come with these associations may also provide some cultural imprints. Think about the cities and towns where you have lived, what schools (K–12 and beyond) you have attended, any post–high school education (where and when), trade/union/fraternity/sorority affiliations, organizations you have worked for or been involved with, military (and the differing service experiences there), government, associations, or private sector employment. Culture involves a great deal of factors that shape one's trajectory, considering race, gender, religion, upbringing, sexual orientation, lifestyle, geographical diversity, politics, social-economic positioning, on onward. All of these may sometimes compensate for a lack of depth in the other Player Capability Index lettered categories, or may dictate that you have to draw deeper on a lettered variable due to a lack of cultural connections or leverage points.

   Culture helps you develop values, beliefs, standards of excellence, and expectations. To better understand your and others' inner trajectory conversations, try to recognize the value-imprints others have. This will usually give you a better understanding of their TC.

8. E = Expectations. The second letter E in the formula, outside the parenthesis, influences all the letters inside the parenthesis. This formula is influenced by the power of the E2 on the outside of the equation. There are two applications of expectation. Your expectations of yourself drive your final performance output, which combines with the expectations of the other party to cause you to pull upon your $T + A + P + E + C$ to attain true peak performance execution effectiveness (or not). You may possess tremendous depth within each of these letters $(T + A + P + E + C)$, but if you have a low set of expectations for yourself in any given situation, you will take your B game (at best) to the office. So expectations really do become the driver to the capability level of an individual. So—is your trajectory calibration based upon your true IP Statement and your desire from the FIST Factor calibrators you need? Or are you being guided aimlessly down trajectories by an ill-fated FIST Factor?

The second element of expectations is that which others have of you. If these two are not in sync, a potential trajectory implosion may be in the making. Many times, others' perceived understanding of your T, P, E, or C dictates their expectations of your capability and the results. You may fail to recognize that you're drawing on your culture too heavily, and there is a lack of training (knowledge), accomplishments, and experience to actually generate results.

We live in a world of assumed expectations; what is clear in your mind is based upon your TC and trajectory shapers, but may not be as clear to another person. So, if it is not written, shared, and acknowledged by the other party(s), you may be heading to a trajectory Point B disappointment!

**9.** R = Relationships. Again, this is the last letter within the formula that drives the DNA of a person (or group) to the final letter R for results. The entire formula is influenced and can be enhanced or diminished on a person's past and present relationships, which influence the development of each DNA variable within the formula. The people that you know can either help build or tear down your Player Capability Index. Leveraged effectively, your relationships can allow you to showcase your inner power; ineffectively utilized, they hinder your best efforts.

The 2 serves to remind us that the first application of relationships which influences a person's capability will be their past and present relationships. To enhance a person's capability level, confidence, and self-initiative see if either of the relationships have had a constructive positive influence on one's trajectory, then increase the same. To change from trajectory B or accelerate one's trajectory C attainment, sometimes taking inventory of the Relationship set in the formula will reveal a need to change up these in this influence category or circle.

Imagine that you had a colleague or employee who was raised with influencers that modeled deception, deceit, and arrogance. It would not be a surprise to have that person take advantage of you and maintain a demeanor of ambivalence. Now imagine a person kicked out of college or someone surrounded by those who have sold their honor for material possessions; it would not be a stretch for that person to hijack your credentials and possessions to further their career or ambitions. Conversely, a person of honor and strong DNA variables can lead you and others to greatness.

If I wanted to get a snapshot of possible trajectory imprint influences upon you, I might look to see who you're connected to via LinkedIn, Facebook, Twitter, your Rolodex, or other social media.

Likewise, this would give me an indication of the influence that you may have upon others.

The insight you gain from this formula will allow you to forecast your own behaviors in good times and crisis situations with a great level of accuracy. So how do you practically apply this to your life? Let's say you have been asked to do something, which becomes letter R (Results) in the formula. In order to determine whether the task is within your X-Factor domain or not, run the other letters within the parenthesis of the formula upon yourself and determine the depth of each letter as it relates to you. The questions that this model raises will reveal the answers to your X-Factor—and the same can be applied to others.

I have worked with countless certified public accountants (CPAs) over the years. Every new year, as federal tax season approaches, most people assume that a CPA is the perfect person to consult with for tax advice. And although a CPA most often does indeed have a formal education in some degree of accounting (Letter T), and has probably worked at some point in their career (Letter P) in an accounting environment, it does not mean that tax advice is every CPA's X-Factor. Many in fact do not actually do taxes, finance, or audits; instead, they use this formula to seek out advice from others that do work daily in these spaces.

People who run their lives without the use of this model are like ships with no navigational systems. Any port is welcome, even though it may be the wrong destination.

A better understanding of the actual responses to each qualifying letter in the above model drives you to better understand your Performance Quotient (PQ) and ultimately your trajectories at any given time and that of others' PQ level. It is the combination of the above IQ and EQ factors that arrive at your PQ.

Imagine if we actually applied this diagnostic instrument to our social networks—those organizations that do business with us as clients, employees, and vendors—to determine which individuals get the opportunity for promotions and which executives ascend upward, who is allowed onto a board of directors and who we elect to public office.

Consider again the Player Capability Index model. Have you ever known someone within organizations, associations, government, and your own personal interactions that possessed a tremendous depth of T yet a crappy A? If so, they do not P very well, do they? Conversely, you probably know people who may not have tremendous depth of T, but who do possess a great A and they at least try to P all the time. That is a trajectory game changer!

In nearly all vocations, the T can be provided—but the A is more difficult to cultivate. Consider how organizations like Southwest Airlines and Harley-Davidson reinvented their industries and why they are market leaders. Both use A as the central factor in determining who they hire and promote.

Here's more evidence of how powerful this model can be. Imagine you were to take the credentials of political candidates in any election (local, state, or federal level) and diagnostically evaluate the resumes without seeing the individuals' names. What you would arrive at is the clear logic-based realization that many times the final candidates to select from fail miserably to be the best candidate to be selected. Far too often we allow our misguided emotional, biased TC to guide our actions; knowing this in advance can be used to predict the actions of ourselves and others.

If that is too big of an example, consider how this works within your organization, or among your co-workers, family, and yourself. Are you beginning to see how the application of each person's FIST Factor calibrators and their respective IP Statements shapes their every action, comment, and belief?

If you want to search for performance execution at the highest level and observe even more clearly what happens when you let emotions and popularity win out over competency, run the Player

Capability Index model on any well-known leader outside of your immediate workplace or community. Many times when you step away from what is familiar to you, you will notice that the people you have assumed to be on top of their game actually elicit some appropriate and powerful questions regarding their capability. Are these the caliber of individuals to take you in the trajectory pathway needed? Most importantly, run the formula on yourself and ask: Would you hire yourself for what you currently do now, knowing these TC ideas?

Performance Execution Stars Always Surround Themselves With UP ... If you were to apply this new matrix, you would always hire up, promote up, and associate up. Would you always ensure that the calibrators in your life are always raising your performance bar? I say, yes!

Recognize greatness and invite it to shine; do not be intimidated by it. The people who are responsible for improving things are frequently easily intimidated by performers. Therefore, instead of running this formula to gauge the level of performance DNA they must apply, they instead surround themselves with people that are inferior to them. This way, they'll always seem superior to everyone else. And when you hire and promote down, you dumb down.

By understanding the Player Capability Index formula, you can objectively recognize where you or others may fail, due to expectations to perform from your actual suc-factor basis. Performance execution and trajectory achievement comes only from playing to and from your X-Factor dominance.

Here are several additional X-Factor, self-propelling, forward momentum action plans, to ensure performance excellence from you and those around you:

1. Look with brutal honesty at your present reality and the future you wish to move toward. Ask yourself if you currently possess or have access to, through your sphere of influence, the human

capital DNA necessary to attain true success. If the answer is no, do not accept the position before you; get people with the real human capital DNA to lead others forward, at that moment in time. Stop letting yourself, your family members, colleagues, employees, and associates in your organization position themselves for failure or mere mediocrity.

2. Make sure the members of your FIST Factor or those you enlist to be your mentors or Peer Accountability Partners, people with substantial Player Capability Index's themselves, can hold you accountable in a constructive manner and are not all clones of one another—since this breeds groupthink. Diversity in gender, ethnicity, generation, competencies, and experience is critical. (Refer to number 3 below for more.)

3. Look at your organization and realize you can begin to forecast future decisions based upon your Player Capability Index findings. Better yet, do not affiliate with groups whose overall equation is so out of balance that they are destined for failure.

4. Recognize that your IQ and EQ form the great reserve of human capital abilities, and ask yourself honestly whether you invest equally in each. Now, the turbo enhancer to all of this is actually your PQ, or Performance Quotient.

5. Engage in 360-degree human capital learning from a mentor. Begin actively investing in others' human capital DNA by mentoring them and building mentoring systems around you for the free, fluid movement of human capital DNA.

Build a real-time human capital inventory of everyone around you that you can instantly access and easily administer for net needs and appropriate assignment tasking. Imagine as a parent, teacher, mentor, manager, or leader if you didn't only know the depth of every person you engaged, but also had a systematic way to know these answers in real-time—that would be an explosive FIST Factor. Imagine being able to type into a system the requirements for something you needed done, and upon hitting ENTER, a list of real-time, legitimate candidates would be presented back to you. The implications here on training, learning and development, tasking and delegating, and succession planning are enormous.

6. Create a human capital development plan, tied into personal needs for you and everyone you influence. Then demand nothing less than total adherence, commitment, and accomplishment.

   As an example, what fiction, trade, text, or instructional books or training programs would be appropriate and in what sequential order to develop your X-Factor needs further? Who could serve as great mentors to challenge, guide, and develop you forward? Think of T and P in the formula as guideposts to what you could do to develop yourself.

7. Find instant human capital endeavors such as the ones detailed here and others to which you can commit. This will ensure that when you finish this course, you are focused forward and do not digress into rearview-mirror activities, negative self-talk, or whining sessions with others.

8. Consider operating like a professional athlete—that is, getting serious about performance improvement and standards. Explore questions such as: What is the likelihood that a professional athlete would have their game performances recorded for immediate feedback by their trainer or coach? What is the likelihood that they may have the same done for the practices? And what about their desire to review the performances of their major competitor? Of course, I am sure you said "yes" or "high" to each question. Start asking for real-time data collection and coaching to really improve your game and lifetime performance!

9. Assess the performance review instrument your team or firm uses and ask yourself if it really tracks the areas of your performance necessary for performance improvement feedback. If not, add them. Consider also how often it's administered. If

you aren't doing this on a monthly basis at minimum, then why not inquire as to how your colleagues, boss, or even external key clients or customers can start to provide you with this valuable information on a more regular basis?

Imagine that you are now in the time machine again. You choose whether to focus on the future and your performance success or to keep flashing back into the rearview mirror. Those that recognize the objective power of the Player Capability Index model and the ramifications of elevating themselves and others around them will find that they make continuous, significant, and meaningful contributions to others, the organizations they serve, and the community around them. These truly are the VIPs that enlarge the contributions to the planet and elevate performance execution to both an art form and a science. These individuals have a hunger to always better what they do and those with whom they associate.

As you reflect upon the performance of yourself and those around you, do you see players and organizations thriving and embracing objective diagnostic evaluation of individual capability levels? Or do you see complacency as the norm?

This is exactly what Louis Gerstner learned in attaining higher levels of performance execution. As discussed in Chapter 4, Gerstner quickly realized within a short time of arriving at American Express that he was, in large part, in his suc-factor—and that it was much more likely that many of the individuals on his leadership team would demonstrate what their success factors were if he gave them the chance to shine. So it is speculated that he initiated a dialogue about what the team thought should be done to turn the organization around. After a series of conversations, he stood and simply said, "Let's do it."

Gerstner realized that when you are in your suc-factor, you don't need to prove it; rather, you defer to those around you, who would be in their success factor, and realize performance execution as the net result.

With the integration of only the first two performance execution ideas/technologies, all can attain greater efficiency and effectiveness. Imagine your self-talk now when considering these two questions:

1. Does this play to my X-Factor—or, will I suc at this?
2. When tasking others: Does this play to your X-Factor strength, or am I setting you up to 'suc'?"

The PCI formula, $C = (T2 + A + P + E + C)E2 \times R = R$, goes beyond EQ (the attitude-driven variables, also shaped by experiences and culture) and mere IQ (the training variables also laid against the application of what you have performed, and thus accomplished, along with the experience variables) to deliver a clear snapshot of what your PQ can become.

Organizations and associations must prepare individuals and hold them accountable to be VIPs. As presented earlier in this chapter, focus your energies first on your A-level players; these are your leaders, or the people with the capacity to be leaders. Then focus your same energies on your B-level players, as any organization must have a back-fill of great contributors, workers, team members, and employees, and this is where you will find them.

You must constantly evaluate sequential developmental programs, experiences, jobs, interactions, and certifications to ensure that they meet present needs and have projected or forecasted future needs. By utilizing the Player Capability Index diagnostic instrument, individuals can work more objectively and thoroughly in a greater PQ direction.

VIPs live for X-Factor development; these are opportunities to showcase and to apply their strength base. They seemingly reenergize themselves by growing their and others' X-Factor baselines through individual Player Capability Index development. By using this formula as an overlay, you can examine those people from whom you seek counsel, advice, or mentorship to ensure that they "plus" you where you have a deficit. Examine the members of your FIST Factor to recognize their hidden talents that you can gain from, learn from, and develop from. Now put concerted conscious energy in play to enhance your trajectory and TC.

This formula empowers you to take control of your personal and professional development along the trajectories you desire. Always be mindful of your Point C destinations. There will be sequential goals along your Trajectory C that you can plot to benchmark your progress and ensure you are always on track. Assuming that someone else, or your organization, will take responsibility for this is an abdication of power. It's your job to grow within your position, to calibrate your horizontal and vertical track development, and strategically think through the succession pathway.

I applied this formula for success during a five-hour conversation around organizational effectiveness as a leader (of others or yourself) with former governor Brian Schweitzer (D-MT). To put the learning opportunity into perspective, Schweitzer had been the only two-term governor at the time. He had never held prior elected office. During his two terms, he achieved positive state economic business growth, a balanced yearly budget, and maintained an annual fiscal cash surplus (for eight consecutive years 2004–2012)—all during a time when the nation was in economic crisis and experiencing staggering unemployment.

On our flight back from Washington, D.C., Schweitzer and I engaged in a conversation about his entry point into politics. As a farmer and rancher, he understands the process of business and "keeping some grain back each year"—which is just how he approached state government. He recognized and applied his growing up on a farm, college education, work in the Middle East after college, and work back in the United States, all of which were imprints on how he thinks, acts, and operates.

When Schweitzer became governor, he was presented with a list for new vehicles to be ordered as a routine action. So, in getting the state's fiscal house in order, he asked for a list of all state vehicles. No one could produce the report, so he froze all future fleet orders. He explained that, on the ranch, they drive vehicles for many years if they work, and so too will the state. The same was true for new computers and computer systems; once he learned that most were used for e-mails, processing paperwork, and looking up phone numbers, he halted routine purchase of new computers. And the same for retail commercial office space—as a major renter throughout the state in an imploding economy, he called for all leases to be renegotiated to real market value terms.

Schweitzer's approach illuminates his ability to motivate others to take ownership of their areas of responsibility and draw upon their Player Capability Index abilities to perform. With an objective model like this, you can hold yourself accountable to sound decision-making and specifically determine where others need to be drawn upon for greatness—and where you can hold them accountable.

The Player Capability Index formula helps you recognize where your deficits are and engage thought-leaders, mentors, and experts to develop your talents further. This matrix prompts you to utilize, track, and hold yourself accountable for the sequential and psychological flow of your trajectory developmental needs. It will guide you in mapping out a career pathway and exploring how to design positions that allow you to amplify your talents and move from success to significance in everything you do.

---

### Redo You—The Line: *Your Trajectory Code*™ Calibrators/Windshield Application Time:

In order to manage your Line and ensure your trajectory growth and development, you as the reader must assume ownership of the calibrations that take place. You must address any issues that influence your personal trajectory growth, peer-to-peer interactions, or hinder your Line, and assume ownership of your professional organizational

*(continued)*

(*continued*)

trajectory advancement. Answer the following three questions to give you perspective on where you are on your Line.

1. **Personal (Positional) Growth:** Where are you now at Point A? Where are you on your Line based upon what you are doing? Is your trajectory headed toward Point B or Point C? What specific actions must you implement in the next 7/30/60 days to ensure your vocational positional trajectory pathway aims toward Point C?

   _____

   _____

2. **Peer-to-Peer Influence Accountability:** Where are you now? What is Point A? How are Lines intersecting based upon what you are doing and how others are interacting with you? Is your trajectory headed toward Point B or Point C? What specific actions must you implement in the next 7/30/60 days with a Peer Accountability Partner to ensure your trajectory pathway aims toward Point C?

   _____

   _____

3. **Organizational Growth:** Where are you now? What is Point A? Based on what you are doing, is your trajectory headed toward Point B or Point C? What specific actions must you implement in the next 7/30/60 days to ensure that your trajectory pathway within your organization moves you toward Point C needs?

   _____

   _____

*Trajectory Calibration*

# CHAPTER 6

# Applying PFC FISHES to Your Life Trajectory for Balance and Inner Harmony

You learned in earlier chapters how to apply the FIST Factor model as a tool to create positive personal influencers for your Line and enhance your individual performance. It's equally critical to convey outward behaviors, such as posture and word choice, that express a positive attitude. Assessing the voices you allow into your head determines the level of performance execution you and others can attain and the ultimate trajectory direction you can experience.

You are the sum whole of every influencer you have allowed into your subconscious mind throughout your entire life. These influencers have guided you in assessing every situation, encounter, person, and opportunity. They calibrate your TC and dictate your performance execution.

Think of it this way: Visualize a teeter-totter. One side contains all of the positive, constructive, nurturing influencers. These are the voices you hear whenever you consider doing or saying anything. They are processed in a nanosecond, and are reflected in what you say or do out loud.

Conversely, the other side of the teeter-totter represents all of the negative, destructive, whining influencers. These voices are processed immediately and also speak to you whenever you consider doing or saying anything.

The side of the teeter-totter that is weighted down more within an individual, organization, or group, influences their collective TC and the level of performance experienced. So, imagine what your FIST Factor does to your internal teeter-totter. Which way does it tend to lean the most? That is a significant trajectory calibration clue.

In order to clarify how this works, imagine the brain from a business perspective (see Figure 6.1). The left side of the diagram represents the frontal section of the performance brain, known as the neocortex. It processes new data and is the learning center of the brain.

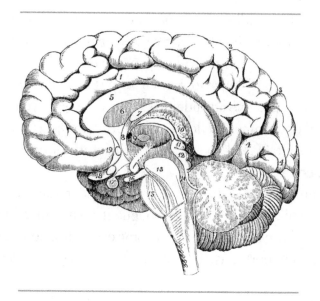

**FIGURE 6.1   The Whole Brain Model**

Visually, you can recognize this space as the smaller of the two sides. The back side, or right side of the diagram, is significantly larger, and the performance execution star understands and manages this accordingly. Stanford University, which has volumes of data on brainwave management, suggests that the front side or the conscious brain we use is merely 6 to 17 percent of our brain matter. This section is shut off when you sleep. To leverage your inner energies and assure that the trajectory you are on makes sense, start by recognizing what you mentally feed your subconscious and who is on your FIST Factor, because they work 24/7 on your trajectory direction.

Whether you read about Tour de France star Lance Armstrong (from his racing career to the yellow bracelet craze, and from his foundation for cancer research to the court of public opinion, you see the manifestation of his TC), golf phenomenon Tiger Woods (his rise, fall, and the rebirth of his TC), Olympic swimming sensation Michael Phelps, perennial investor Warren Buffett, or serial business entrepreneurs Richard Branson or Oprah Winfrey, you'll notice that what each has in common is what occupies their mental teeter-totter. It directly impacts their self-talk and mental life balance.

Conversely, when we look at those who do not play to their X-Factor, refuse to grow their Player Capability Index™ and do not have a sound IP Statement, we're compelled to ask, "How often is the right side of the brain heading to the trajectory desired?" The right side of the diagram represents the rear section of the performance brain, known as the limbic system—the region of the brain where:

1. Memories are stored.
2. Habits radiate outward.
3. Emotions are birthed.

You'll notice that all three are factors shaped and reinforced by your FIST Factor and IP Statement.

We draw upon the larger, back side of the brain to guide our behaviors. This is how the teeter-totter concept can guide your performance levels both in the present and for future efforts. And if you know what occupies an individual or organization's teeter-totter, you can forecast actions. If a person has disproportionately more suc-factors on their teeter-totter (which represent the back side of the brain) then lack of performance execution will be the reality. If there are more positives, then performance execution success will be attained—the limbic system is the key.

Imagine individuals and organizations that play to the negative individuals, and not the transformers. These are the individuals and organizations that resist performance execution at the highest levels, and that want to participate in their future based upon past tense teeter-totter variables, instead of seeking out new performance influencers.

## HOW LIFE-BALANCE FACTORS INFLUENCE YOUR MENTAL TEETER-TOTTER AND TRAJECTORY

More often than not, your teeter-totter is comprised of influencers that shape your FIST Factor, your X-Factor tendencies, and your IP Statement, and what you make yourself available to in respect of your Player Capability Index. It is a very specific set of life-balanced influencers that we draw upon and from which our trajectory is influenced and calibrated. In some cases, they are also the forces that create stress and internal conflicts.

There are nine life-balance areas I have come to recognize in both super achievers and disillusioned individuals in life. I call this the PFC FISHES™ model. You can begin to inventory which influencers may consciously or subconsciously be on your teeter-totter, or anyone else's, by recognizing what you know about these life influencers from the following specific areas:

1. **P**rofessional aspects: Job, position, career, industry, vocation, advancement, opportunities.
2. **F**amily aspects: Immediate and extended influencers, parents, grandparents, uncles, aunts, siblings, children, surrogates.
3. **C**ommunity: Direct and indirect aspects, interactions, and involvements.
4. **F**inancial: Stability, earning potentials, debts, capital gains, obligations.
5. **I**nspirational: Internal and external drivers, motivators, self-actualization, emotional supports.
6. **S**ocial: Personal and professional circles of influence, interaction, networking, acceptance or validation by outward sources, intellectual and emotional outlets.
7. **H**ealth and Fitness: Physical balance drivers, exercise opportunities, wellness, and nutritional triggers.
8. **E**ducational: The technical and professional knowledge and training aspects to create sound mind and capacities for self-fulfillment or to give back to one's community.

**9. S**piritual: The drivers for a sound mind-body experience that provide one meaning and purpose, a belief and subscription to higher force.

Let's discuss how to use this model to maintain a balanced teeter-totter of influencers and to recognize when you are over-compensating and allowing the teeter-totter to send you off on a destructive trajectory. The order of the categories does not imply that any one is more important than another; it is merely an acronym to help you remember all of them. All nine categories can dramatically influence your trajectory; therefore, it's critical to be able to reconcile the answers to two important questions below. Those answers will dictate for you when any one category is more important than another and when energy is being invested into any one of the nine categories at an unbalanced level.

Your FIST Factor can reinforce this or take away from the nine factors. Your IP Statement can enhance them and allow you to keep them in perspective and balance; or, it can derail your trajectory. We all face challenges and demands in every one of these areas on any given day. It is these areas that we plan, set goals within, strive toward, and can feel overwhelming pressures within.

You can think of these nine areas as individual wedges in a pie chart—and then answer the following questions:

**Question One**: Please assign each category a percentage point between 0 and 100 that reflects how well you believe you are performing that category area in your life. This will provide a snapshot of how you observe your reality at the present time. An important point: Your categories should not total 100 overall. This is a significant clue as to why many people are stressed and feel out of balance; they are trying to live each category area up to someone else's expectations. This first question will merely allow you to look at each category area independent of the others and assess how well you are executing that category area right now (zero being you suc and 100 being you feel whole).

**Question Two**: More important than the responses to questions are the answers you now assign each wedge category based upon this second round. Please assign each category a number between 0 and 100 that reflects what percentage of your time you should be spending in that category. In this case, your categories *must* total 100.

Many people feel that they'll achieve balance by giving relatively equal numbers to Question One. In fact, balance—a major life trajectory calibrator—comes only when you recognize how important a category is *first*, and then matching the amount of time you spend on it to how important it is. Now you can begin to recalibrate your trajectory to your real balance number.

For an interactive real-time Excel spreadsheet version of the PFC FISHES Life-Balance diagram and grid, e-mail drjeffspeaks@aol.com and request it as a free download.

Imagine now matching up your IP Statement to the teeter-totter influences that can keep you aligned, balanced, and on trajectory for your life goals. You can have goals within each PFC FISHES area and even match up a situational FIST Factor for each area individually. You can also maintain one overall macro FIST Factor to ensure alignment of all your endeavors and efforts!

I am reminded when I reflect back over this matrix of a memory snapshot from my childhood (Family) that still has an influence upon my performance execution DNA today. I would get off the school bus, finish my chores on our pig farm, and go play in the dirt pile adjacent to the pig barn. Now, if you have ever been on a farm, you probably know what the dirt pile really was. But when you're a child, you don't see the crap; you just see the fun. In much the same way, every job has a crap quotient. Performance execution and trajectory success is about working through that, and realizing that there is also a success quotient.

Another moment that had a profound influence on my performance execution DNA was when my high school cross-country coach, Graeme Badger, advised me to attend an out-of-state college after graduation. He noted that in his 20 years of high school teaching, he had noticed that every student that left the state for college grew significantly further in performance execution stature when compared to students that stayed in-state to attend college. Their trajectory was profound. He therefore wanted me to pick a college so far away geographically that I couldn't easily get home every weekend; where I would be forced to stand on my own and not be able to rely on any of the structures or people I would have if I had stayed home. He knew it would be best if I went somewhere that, ideally, I did not know anyone. This would allow me to make my own choices with no teeter-totter guilt or preconceived expectations. By attending a school that was out of my home state, I learned a critical lesson: If you really want to see what performance execution possibilities lie dormant within you, you must go somewhere outside of your teeter-totter norm.

Each of these was a trajectory calibrator before I even realized it. Each set in motion an entirely different Line, created a whole new set of calibrators and trajectory experiences, new FIST Factor members, opportunities to see what my X-Factors could be, to learn the importance of the depth of my Player Capability Index—all before I realized there were formulas to life success.

The dominant influencers on your FIST Factor influence your teeter-totter and are the people you allow on it. To better understand the people around you today—and especially when interacting with the different generational segments in your professional life—start asking which influencers (time, geography, people, experiences, places, responsibilities, social, or entertainment influences) are in your head; and better yet, other people's. I have recognized that it is the balance of the PFC FISHES model, combined with an understanding of the FIST Factor concept, blended with an IP Statement, which peak achievers and high potential individuals maintain.

As presented previously, and at a minimum, there are several very specific types of influencers in your life. This group may include individuals that have passed away, or past interactions—or they may include present physical connections, all serving as internal mental drivers affecting how you:

- See yourself.
- Benchmark yourself against your true physical and mental abilities.
- Conduct internal discussions.
- Outwardly engage others.

Ultimately, the teeter-totter comprised of every past, present, and future positive or negative stimulant calibrates your trajectory and reinforces your TC. As an individual or organization possesses, reinforces, and builds upon its existing TC, it often does not recognize the need for a major TC makeover to regain stability and success. What you will do to change that is:

- Reinforce the sense and purpose for their existence.
- Help them shape their personality, character, and reputation.
- Guide them in uncovering and living their values through their behaviors.
- Reveal which performance standards will be measured and accepted and what will be tolerated.
- Determine self-pride, self-respect, self-dignity, self-worth, and self-belief.
- Uncover others' perceptions and expectations of you.

You'll experience a reduced level of self-imposed stress by calibrating your PFC FISHES categories to be weighted for what you really want. This will keep you from allowing others to dictate to you what each category in *your life* should look like. Then imagine the trajectory success you could experience on a daily basis if your teeter-totter was operating from a balanced state more often than not.

By applying the FIST Factor model as a tool to create positive influencers within, you can enhance individual performance and practice outward behaviors that convey a positive attitude. Taking stock of the voices you allow into your head determines the level of performance execution you and others can attain. Utilizing this architecture allows you to explore what balance in your PFC FISHES model means for you, and allows you to attain greater successes.

Remember: You are the sum whole of every influencer you have allowed into your subconscious mind!

Now by understanding the PFC FISHES model and the inner imprints and dialogue from your FIST Factor, you can recalibrate your trajectory to attain greater rewards from Point C and stop living others' Point B.

---

### Redo You—The Line: *Your Trajectory Code*™ Calibrators/Windshield Application Time:

In order to manage your Line and ensure your trajectory growth and development, you as the reader must assume ownership of the calibrations that take place. You must address any issues that influence your personal trajectory growth, peer-to-peer interactions, or hinder your Line, and assume ownership of your professional organizational trajectory advancement. Answer the following three questions to give you perspective on where you are on your Line.

1. Personal (Positional) Growth: Where are you now at Point A? Where are you on your Line based upon what you are doing? Is your trajectory headed toward Point B or Point C? What specific actions must you implement in the next 7/30/60 days to ensure your vocational positional trajectory pathway aims toward Point C?

_____

_____

_____

_____

*(continued)*

*(continued)*

**2.** Peer-to-Peer Influence Accountability: Where are you now? What is Point A? How are Lines intersecting based upon what you are doing and how others are interacting with you? Is your trajectory headed toward Point B or Point C? What specific actions must you implement in the next 7/30/60 days with a Peer Accountability Partner to ensure your trajectory pathway aims toward Point C?

_____

_____

_____

_____

**3.** Organizational Growth: Where are you now? What is Point A? Based on what you are doing, is your trajectory headed toward Point B or Point C? What specific actions must you implement in the next 7/30/60 days to ensure that your trajectory pathway within your organization moves you toward Point C needs?

_____

_____

_____

_____

*Trajectory Calibration*

# CHAPTER 7

# Shift Happens ... Trajectory Shift Drivers and Bridges That Create Sustained Positive Change

Of course, no matter how well you plan, major life changes occur that can significantly shift your trajectory. Some happen in such a subtle manner that you fail to recognize them—that is, until you find yourself well underway to Point B, while your intended trajectory was Point C. It is critical to be aware of every action and whether you are, at all times, en route to your intended trajectory point.

It is critical to establish accountability mechanisms to assist you—whether these are self-imposed, electronic, peer-administered mentors, or facilitated by strategic members of your FIST Factor (what may also be called your Master Mind. MasterMind, what napoleon Hill in his classic work THAN AND GROW RICH referred to as a MasterMind group.). It's human nature to resist change, especially if that change is perceived as significant; but you can alter your trajectory toward the positive, by mere 1 percent calibration adjustments.

Trajectory shift drivers do not have to be complex to yield great results. Ockham's razor, a principle attributed to the fourteenth-century English philosopher William of Ockham, states that "Entities should not be multiplied beyond necessity; that one should choose the simplest explanation, that one requiring the fewest assumptions and principles." Many times we make various instances of change, trauma, or other issues into more than they need to be. If we could just simplify, we'd find more effective strategies and tactics to trajectory success.

Understanding these simple shift drivers in both personal and professional application is essential to sustained trajectory success. In the past few generations, we have altered our inherent entrepreneurial success trajectory by subtle shift driver changes, although at times explained—or more likely excused away—if to no one else but ourselves, as appropriate. However, we failed to recognize the intermediate and long-term trajectory ramifications.

For example, when I listen to most people today talk, I conclude that when I was a child, I had it rough!

I was expected to get up early every morning to make my bed, get washed and dressed, and do chores before getting on a bus for school. I was expected to be mindful of my classmates and teachers in school, come home and do chores and homework, all before dinner. If I acted out of line, my parents had already given permission to my teachers and administrators to spank me—and I would receive the same treatment upon arriving home. If there ever was an academic problem in school, I owned it; it was never blamed on ineffective teachers or an administrator. All would work together to correct any problems, with my active participation. It's clear how much of this has changed by today's standards.

Those are just some of the shift triggers that made me and other members of my generation—children of the 1950s through the 1970s—who we are. But that story has since ceased being accurate in the past 30 years as the next generations are being raised with few to none of those trajectory-shaping forces. Moreover, that cascades through the entire TC architecture, that individuals or a society possesses.

Both the Society for Human Resource Management (SHRM) and the Association for Talent Development (ATD; formerly the American Society for Training & Development [ASTD]) within their annual human resource surveys agree that the top workplace challenges with workers today are (1) lack of work ethic, (2) lack of self accountability and structure, and (3) complete breakdown in discipline and lack of consequences for self-actions.

Now reflect upon what your Line telegraphs to others. Does any of this apply to you?

When you recognize the trajectory-shaping influences on your life and the Line you have been on since the day you were born, you'll see that these are the trajectory forces that have shaped your TC. Recognizing this and identifying whether what are doing works for the trajectory you seek will determine your next steps. If you realize that the TC imprint will not allow you to get from where you are—from Point A to your intended Point Cs in life—you can become empowered to start to making calculated trajectory changes and expose yourself to appropriate shift drivers that have meaning.

You must create a Line in order to prompt the psychology for change in yourself and others. The specific action steps or shift drivers undertaken to recalibrate your behaviors will be self-evident. However, as a way to help you brainstorm, there is a detailed list of starting shift drivers to help you create a more self-directed entrepreneurial trajectory later in this section.

But first, let's set the framework for change. When you find yourself along Point B pathway and need to shift to a Point C trajectory, that transition will require a bridge. In order for you, or anyone else, to participate by crossing that bridge, the shift drivers you deploy must follow this chronological psychological order for greatest acceptance and the least resistance:

1. Awareness: You become aware of a need, a shift, and the fact that trajectory change is essential. You recognize that your present trajectory is not working, that outcomes could be better or worse if a trajectory is explored or not, or that you must alter or abandon the path you are on. Only at this point will you or anyone else entertain any new trajectory ideas, actions, changes, or adjustments in life, and the same for your FIST Factor or even an understanding of Player Capability Index adjustments.

2. Intervention: You explore a specific and measurable trajectory action plan; make a change in behavior, response, or reaction to a situation that will alter your trajectory and place you on a more appropriate and sustainable pathway for success.

3. Commitment: You embrace your desire and follow through to a new action plan and trajectory for which you are willing to assume ownership for.

So what happens when you encounter those shift drivers we discussed at the chapter's opening? Believe it or not, though frequently unexpected and unwelcome, these can be blessings in disguise, creating instant solutions and entrepreneurial trajectory energy for you and those around you.

Understanding that bridge and recognizing that there are endless engagement strategies for transitioning yourself or others from Point B to C will empower you to take action, or assist others in doing so. Just as Point A is calibrated by your goals, objectives, and driven by the values within one, that in turn drive what vision a person or organization may have, all of this culminates the in language that is used. Point C should have very clearly defined language so that you and all parties involved know all along pathway C trajectory whether they are aligned or falling out of calibration and sliding towards trajectory B at any given time. Here are 21 powerful ways to create a culture of forward-moving, solution-oriented trajectory for yourself and your colleagues.

1. **Become proficient with D = C + L:** Engage in dialogue with others via effective outbound signal-sending communication and effective internal listening of signals. Remember: The ability to communicate interactively with another party means initiating an effective dialogue, or exchange. And that requires the ability to send a signal to the other party through effective communication coupled with effective listening, thus the inbound comprehension of the signal you send to them and the signal (communication) they send to you, hence D = C + L.

2. **Become an entrepreneurial leader:** Look inward for new ways of doing what have been the traditional trajectories; explore alternative paths for delivering your ideas, services, and deliverables in a better, faster, more cost-effective manner, or a uniquely different form.

3. **Expand your job responsibilities:** This will allow to play to your own Player Capability Index strengths and achieve a more profound X-Factor for the benefit of others.

4. **Cross-learn:** Have a functioning understanding of the people and positions in any system prior to and after your actions. Knowing to some degree what the people before and after do with your work product will empower you to improve your trajectory, and perhaps theirs as well.

5. **Networking and personal tagline:** Stop and reflect on your IP Statement. This serves as a great conversational reference point to use to convey in a few short sentences who you are and what your trajectory is.

6. **Request feedback with action plans:** Be hungry for performance feedback to improve your future trajectories when opportunities present themselves. This will encourage you to solicit feedback from your FIST Factor or individuals you feel you can learn from. Make sure that you aren't merely seeking positive affirmation for your endeavors. The idea is to drill deeper for actual behavioral-based feedback on how to elevate your performance and trajectory the next time. Ask for who, what, when, where, why, and how data points to improve.

7. **Offer feedback with action plans:** In much the same way you seek it in number six, be willing to provide performance feedback to improve others' future trajectories when opportunities present themselves. Again, make sure you don't just offer positive affirmation, but impart actual behavioral-based feedback. This is the only way they will elevate their performance and trajectory the next time. Give the same kind of information you're seeking—who, what, when, where, why, and how data points.

8. **Volunteer strategically, internally, and externally:** Reduce your life-balance stress (PFC FISHES model reference) and increase your value to others by recognizing

where your depth of Player Capability Index factors are and where your true X-Factor is—and let that be your new Line. This trajectory-calibrating clue will help show you when you should volunteer and where to volunteer within the organizations, business enterprises, departments/divisions/teams, virtual enterprises, and associations you associate with. These opportunities will accelerate your trajectory toward Point C and further successes in life.

9. **Identify gaps-n-cracks:** Look around you for places where you can apply your talents due to lack of appropriate Player Capability Index levels of others being applied to needs. Then bring that forth and execute.

10. **Identify 1 Percent Factors©:** As discussed earlier, your trajectory direction can be best modified and amplified by identifying the simple 1 percent trajectory adjustments that can produce significant Point C attainment.

11. **Dress:** Remember that you will never get a second chance to make that first impression. People begin to calibrate their impression of you based upon first interactions—so your appearance counts. Make sure you are dressed the part for the role you want to execute. You can always dress down to any given situation, but you can never dress up once you have arrived. What you wear and how you present yourself reveals how you see yourself and the level of self-respect, pride, and dignity that you carry internally.

12. **Mirror effectively:** Learn to moderate yourself in the presence of others to make them feel more aligned with you. If they are more thoughtful in their language, you become more thoughtful. If they talk slower or faster, adjust to be in pace with them. For example, I tend to have a fast communication pace; so I must remind myself to slow down to be more effective when speaking with another person who is taking their time, and thus mirror their pace. If I am interacting with a

person that is more social, outgoing, and likes stories as they talk, then I mirror them more by doing some of the same.

13. **Learn to forecast:** Draw upon your Player Capability Index to share foresight without living in a place of hindsight frustrations. Share liberally to accelerate others success along their lines as well.

    For instance, I often find myself in an environment where the subject-matter expert for a need or topic is away and the remaining colleagues are not as expert in the given material. The problem is worsened when one of the remaining team members knew that the go-to colleague was planning to be away. He or she could have proactively learned how to do more or let their leadership team know about this need in advance. Simply looking ahead in this way saves us a lot of trouble.

    Another example occurs when people have done a job well for many years, but suddenly find themselves unemployed or not getting promoted. This is frequently due to the fact that their proficiencies are no longer needed, and they did nothing to keep their skills cutting-edge and future-focused to be relevant both today and tomorrow.

14. **Integrate strategically into teams:** Consider all that you know and how the TC ideologies presented thus far can guide your inner dialogue as you engage within any dynamic group you are in now or may encounter in the future. Instead of living in guilt by association situations, make it success by association situations!

15. **Vertical and Horizontal Action Information Grams©:** Look for any chance after a significant victory or discovery that can shorten others' trajectories toward success and present those victories from an abundance mentality upward/vertically (white paper, e-mail, brief, digital broadcast, etc.) to all key stakeholders (leaders, managers, clients, bosses). Duplicate those behaviors. If you are a collaborative

participant with others in such victories, ensure that credit is given as appropriate.

16. **Invest in yourself and strategically share weekly:** Always keep an eye out for formal and informal opportunities to add to the depth of each category within the Player Capability Index. Remember that the confused brain cannot get you out of difficult situations; you must take your head to a new level. Inventory the appropriate mental DNA gains for your over-all development or any specific trajectory need. For example, consider the quality and quantity of nonfiction books read in the past month, or magazines/journals with more content than pictures you have read, or the online or television content you have mentally consumed that enriches your mental DNA. Or ask yourself how many self-study or developmental resources have you initiated participating in over the past month, which are not connected to a certification minimum requirement or boss tasked undertaking.

    Once gained, ensure that it does not just take up your mental space. Always look for ways to share back to others what you have learned in an action-oriented way. For example, if your mentor shares something with you, send them back a brief with your top take-away and top learned items. This allows the other person to learn from the interactive relationship as well, and also gives them clarity for their next interaction with you!

17. **Always make the boss look good:** Remember the people (customer, boss, spouse, etc.) that have some trajectory influence on your attaining Point C more efficiently should never be surprised, embarrassed, or let down by your actions. Understand their minimum expectations from you and always exceed them.

18. **ID your USF×2×4:** Just as the marketing world has learned to position and market their deliverables (whether tangible or

intangible) by the USF×2 formula, you should calibrate your trajectory according to these variables. USF 1 means to position yourself based upon your Unique Selling Feature: What do you have to offer that others can't? You must then deploy USF 2, your Unique Service Feature: How you do what you do is what differentiates you from others and gives others cause to associate with you. This will ideally enable your trajectory pathway to yield greater successes. Now, you have four ways to differentiate yourself from others in each of these USFs. If your objective here is to exploit your trajectory shift drivers that create sustained positive change, then always be looking at ways to draw upon your ability to, first, be *better*, second, be *faster* (more efficient), third, be measurably *different*, or fourth, be more *cost-effective* than any other market options. Together, these elements increase your value and position you as the person to come to.

19. **Get out of The Presenter's Box©:** To disarm potential distracters and naysayers, recognize that many times you actually create a trajectory that prompts others to challenge your intended positive ideas. Be aware of this when you stand before a group to share a new or potentially trajectory-changing idea. Know that the first person to say something is typically the person that fights you and your ideas. Now you find yourself having to defend yourself, for it is as if there were imaginary lines on the ground, that you as the presenter are trapped within The Presenter's Box.

To generate trajectory shift drivers for a sustained positive change in these situations, stop defending your views, ideas, statements, and yourself. Shift the negative energy around by inviting the person interrupting you conversationally into the conversation with alternative viable cogent ideas. When the person is finished, politely look at them and say something like, "I appreciate your interest. If you feel that this idea won't work, then let's explore several other options or ideas. Given your background on this topic, what do you feel are some other viable options?" Now let them either respond by making another comment, or actually putting forth ideas for conversation and discussion. You have now invited them to take the rope and work together to pull everyone forward.

20. **Invite plural solutions (x3):** To generate greater and potentially healthier ideas for Point C attainment, ensure that you always have plural options to select from before initiating action. Many times, we hastily move forth with just one idea at time of implementation, for the sake of just getting started. But with no backup plans or trajectories, we can run into problems.

    You always want to have at least three ideas to work from before making any decisions. If addressing a problem with a group of people, I would ask for three or four ideas before I ever start judging any one of them or even providing any response. By putting some conversational distance between when the idea comes up and when you come back to start discussing each in greater detail, the idea's value—or lack thereof—will speak for itself and others will dismiss or accept it accordingly.

21. **Challenging and difficult people:** The more solid and healthy your TC becomes, the greater number of truth tellers you have on your FIST Factor, and the more likely your trajectories will cross with people that have unhealthy TC and destructive FIST Factors.

In working with individuals, whether in a professional situation or personal encounter, I have found that the normal path of people is to accelerate upward in their belief of right and wrong. It is not always that either party is wrong when we have a disagreement with another person or group of people. It is just that when you back up, you are reminded of where you started and where you are intending to go, which serves as a reminder that you have gotten off track. Knowing how to engage people more effectively to be able to bridge from Point B to Point C is essential to trajectory success.

Several years ago, I wrote a book entitled *Enough Already: The 50 Fastest Ways to Deal With, Manage and Eliminate Negativity at Work and Home.* In it, I put forth detailed strategies and techniques for engaging and eliminating these kinds of individuals. One way to start is to consult with your FIST Factor to determine if in fact you are an active participant in the problem. Are you potentially more responsible for the problems, given what you now know about your TC, IP Statement, and FIST Factor? If so, you can make instant trajectory changes. If these objectives are not based on accurate identifiers, then make some tough trajectory 1 percent decisions right now, that when extrapolated will dramatically alter your trajectory away from Point B and onto Point C destinations.

Start by Limiting Your Exposure to difficult people; make yourself legitimately unavailable and overcommitted in other trajectory directions away from them. Likewise, if you can over-task them with legitimate trajectory actions, you will limit their exposure to yourself and others. This will clarify their responsibilities, and you can then hold them accountable for those responsibilities. This will leave them no idle or free time to drive others crazy. Be conscious of the words you use, the tone of your voice, and your every action in their presence, as it does not take much with some people to send them off on the wrong trajectory.

As you now encounter any life changer—minimal or significant—that has the potential to shift your trajectory, you can deploy your TC, FIST Factor, and IP Statement to increase your trajectory effectiveness toward Point C destinations.

All of the above shift drivers can serve as trajectory calibration at Point A. Within the initial launch of any trajectory within the circled area (see Figure I.1), we have identified where the 1 percent calibrations and recalibrations occur as the self-management, self-accountability, self-respect, and the self-success orientation begins. Hopefully you recognize that even little 1 percent interventions, whether self-imposed or on behalf of others, do not have to be complex to yield great results. Remember: Shift happens and the difference between what people would see as success in individuals and organizations is the shift that is recognized in advance and deployed effectively. To do so demonstrates a clear Identity-Purpose Statement, a clear and understandable FIST Factor (with limited or eliminated negative members), and an always evolving relevant constructive Trajectory Code from you as an individual or you as an organization.

Your trajectory destinations are measured by actions, not words.

---

### Redo You—The Line: *Your Trajectory Code*™ Calibrators/Windshield Application Time:

In order to manage your Line and ensure your trajectory growth and development, you as the reader must assume ownership of the calibrations that take place. You must address any issues that influence your personal trajectory growth, peer-to-peer interactions, or hinder your Line, and assume ownership of your professional organizational trajectory advancement. Answer the following three questions to give you perspective on where you are on your Line.

**1.** Personal (Positional) Growth: Where are you now at Point A? Where are you on your Line based upon what you are doing? Is your trajectory headed toward Point B or Point C? What specific actions must you implement in the next 7/30/60 days to ensure your vocational positional trajectory pathway aims toward Point C?

_____

_____

_____

_____

**2.** Peer-to-Peer Influence Accountability: Where are you now? What is Point A? How are Lines intersecting based upon what you are doing and how others are interacting with you? Is your trajectory headed toward Point B or Point C? What specific actions must you implement in the next 7/30/60 days with a Peer Accountability Partner to ensure your trajectory pathway aims toward Point C?

_____

_____

_____

_____

**3.** Organizational Growth: Where are you now? What is Point A? Based on what you are doing, is your trajectory headed toward Point B or Point C? What specific actions must you implement in the next 7/30/60 days to ensure that your trajectory pathway within your organization moves you toward Point C needs?

_____

_____

_____

_____

_Trajectory Calibration_

# CHAPTER 8

# Understanding— and Fixing—the Gap between Lines for Trajectory Realignment

In the same way that organizations do, individuals must understand the Gap between Point B and Point C. This is what helps them recognize what work, action plans, matrices, accountability mechanisms, alliances, and commitment are necessary to bridge that Gap—and then to get back onto a healthy trajectory. Though this can be a very painful experience, understanding how to chart the bridging Lines to get back on track is critical to generating meaningful ROI (return on investment).

The faster an individual can recognize leaving Point A that they are off trajectory C route, off track in essence, and what they are doing if extrapolated outward in a time sequence of immediate future time needs and time frames, or intermediate or long-term time frames will cause ever increasing problems. Then look for the immediate bridges that can be created and deployed to recalibrate to trajectory C success. The longer one waits to create and deploy a bridge, the further outward on trajectory B pathway one becomes, the greater the work will be to re-align and get back on trajectory C endeavors and the greater the resistance will be from others.

It is useless to look back and contemplate what could have been, should have been, or might have been. Any Gap makes it clear that 1 percent calibration and recalibration opportunities closer to Point A in the circled zone (see Figure I.1) were missed. However, it is a very valuable exercise to figure out how you went off trajectory and arrived at the Gap. These trajectory misfires never happen by accident, and the reasons for going off trajectory or the reasons other players in an endeavor go off trajectory lie within your own inner dialogue.

Gaps can appear in a variety of different places and forms:

- **You**: Your position evolves to a point where one day you realize that you did not keep your Player Capability Index relevant, updated, and cutting-edge. As a result, you are unable to deliver what you need to—either in a relationship, or for a client or an employer. You are at Point B and the market needs you to be at Point C.

- **Them:** Your human capital talent pool evolves and ages to a point where one day you realize the impending exodus of a significant player or players. You have not implemented succession planning to fill these positions with potential candidates for replacement or promotion, and have failed to do so throughout your human capital pipeline (from recruitment to on-boarding career pathways to retirement). No amount of venture capital, legacy funding, government bailouts/subsidies, union mandates or challenges, or government regulations to demand employment dictates changes the reality. You are at Point B and the organizations and market needs you to be at Point C.

- **Us:** Whatever deliverable you represent, manufacture, market, deliver, service, or support—whether product or service, tangible or intangible—one day is no longer in as much demand. The market has passed you by; yet you still have all of your trajectory energy behind what no one really wants anymore and the impending financial crisis is great. No amount of venture capital, legacy funding, or government bailouts/subsidies changes the reality. You are at Point B and the market is yelling for you to be at Point C.

- **Rhetoric**: You allow yourself to get caught up in the classic deflection game of rhetoric. This happens when an active participant guides you off of Point C trajectory for their own individualist self-absorbed goals at others' ultimate expense. They use their words to stimulate your emotions and get you off focus and off track. Then you wake up one day at Point B alarmed at how it could be so. You played along the game pathway and passively allowed the Gap to develop and caused the pain-point at which you are now located.

- **Personal habits:** People frequently become so comfortable in their ways and courses of daily actions that intermediate or long-term ramifications of their trajectory are the last things on their mind. With the lack of a balanced and healthy FIST Factor to serve as accountability players or internal thought-leaders to keep you on trajectory pathway C, you can easily find yourself at Point B—a loud wake-up call.

- **Time creates us, good or bad:** The longer you do something a specific way, the more commonplace and expected it becomes, and eventually it takes on its own standard operating procedure (SOP). Sooner or later, everyone associated with this task or habit becomes complacent and unwittingly adopts a mindset of expectation. As time progresses, the task's original intent—the reason we started doing it in the first place—moves further away from what we currently want or need. Is there, for example, a form your colleagues are filling out that is no longer necessary to your current business processes? Is there a standing meeting you've always had that could easily be covered with an e-mail or phone call?

- **Culture:** Culture (e.g., organizational, professional, ethnic, regional or geographical, social, economic, political, personal, religious, generational, etc.) is a powerful Gap creator and can make for very volatile conversation. As we know, the way you were raised has a direct imprint upon your TC, FIST Factor, and windshield versus rearview-mirror operations. This then influences your trajectory and your development of your IP Statement, which reinforces what you will be consciously open to accepting, and what you are likely to reject. For example, people in the 1960s and 1970s were raised in a universal culture in America—taught to value accountability, and strong work ethic. During that time, high school graduation rates were higher, crimes rates were lower, employment rates were higher, and there was simply a greater sense of respect for others. Once you start second-guessing your culture and making allowances for deviations to merely please people, your trajectory will wobble off track quickly. Culture is a calibrator to trajectory actions. We get what we excuse away and tolerate.

- **Education:** Whether your trajectory needs are trade- or vocation-directed or formal and advanced, education is a major calibrator to one's Player Capability Index and serves as a trajectory force for success and viability. In 2012, a Pew Research Center research project in the United States revealed that while there were more than 3 million available jobs in a time when the world and the United States were posting historical unemployment, there was a Gap between the education needed for these jobs and the human capital available. In fact, the Pew report indicated the generation reaching age 30 in 2012 had less than eight months' education post–high school, on average, than the same age generation before them.

Once you determine which of these categories your Gap falls into—and there may be more than one—you can begin the heavy lifting to bridge the Gap and get back onto trajectory course C. You can also work to elude Gaps in the future by realigning and simultaneously tracking what the Gap is/was and how that Gap came about. You can design an action plan that helps you avoid a particular Gap in the future. Many times it is the lack of experience that allows some Gaps to develop. Or perhaps it's the emergence of new endeavors, markets, or deliverables for which you failed to consider short- and long-term extrapolations.

Individuals and organizations must understand the Gap between Point B and Point C, and recognize that you do not just arrive at Point B, nor do you just arrive at Point C. To bridge that Gap and get back onto trajectory pathway C requires that you and others be able to engage in a serious, tough discussion of solutions, with no rhetoric and finger pointing. Everyone participated in the actions that led you to arrive at Point B.

I recently worked with a financial institution that recognized the impending loss of senior management and leadership individuals in their business over the course of an upcoming five-year period. In response to this coming loss, they had developed a comprehensive leadership development program to touch the next generation of potential leaders in their firm. In bringing them together monthly, I asked how confident the senior leadership team was in these identified next-generation individuals' working knowledge of the overall business. They responded that they felt that everyone had solid overall knowledge. However, once we did some surveying, we realized that almost every next-generation leader had adequate knowledge of their work area, some knowledge of the business unit or area immediately connected to them, and very low to no knowledge on all other areas and business units in the organization. A significant gap was identified, and a solution was implemented as an integral part of the leadership development program.

For another example, run the Player Capability Index upon yourself. Use that data as an overlay to your profession or job, and ask yourself if are you missing any letter T or P relevant to yourself or a valuable employee in your industry, either now or projected out five years from now. Anything you may be missing is a gap for you, and by recognizing that now you can project forward on needs and work to attain them, to be relevant for tomorrow's Point B.

To move forward *and* address the Gaps and design solutions individually or as a group, apply the FIST Factor model as a tool to create positive influencers. Then use that energy to return to your IP Statement (and in a group dynamic that would mean going back to the organization's mission statements) as a baseline (Point A). While sophisticated matrix and decision software can be utilized and even considered for post analysis and benchmarking endeavors, an immediate trajectory recalibrator for realignment and forward movement once again is the simplest route.

The STOPS™ model is a great way to determine how you have gotten to Point B—and how you can bridge the gap back to Point C. This is an effective, systematic way of facilitating decision making and getting back into execution mode and Point C trajectory pathway activities.

There are only four psychological steps to making a decision. The STOPS model allows you to objectively facilitate the process to bridge the Gap and ensure forward thoughtful movement by following five sequential steps:

1. **S = Stop and See what the issue is that you must address.** Recognize what the Gap is really about, and ensure you are not addressing symptoms of the Gap but the actual Gap. A quick way to tell that you've addressed this and all other steps at a detailed level is to identify the who, what, when, where, why, and how data points.

   You can see how the S step here served business leaders and yourself in the two previous examples by building a more comprehensive leadership development program and by ensuring that you have the talent set to meet future market and employment needs.

2. **T = Target and Think through why that issue is worthy of discussion and attention.** Determine its relevance and who owns that issue; these are the individuals who should be involved in these steps and whose ownership cannot be excused. Identify where the trajectory went off track, what led to Point B, what the steps were and which players participated in the trajectory mis-calibrations. Once you've completed this analysis, move on to Step 3.

3. **O = Organize Options as to how to address the S and always ensure your multiple options at this step.** Consider alternative actions and solutions before engaging in a conversation of viability and selection. To scope out ideas, ask yourself if each participant in the conversation has contributed or if you have weighed the S and the T against each member of your FIST Factor for more ideas and options. Make sure you

evaluate the implementation steps sequentially; this will help you figure out how to lose the Gap and get back onto pathway Point C. Recognize who the critical stakeholders will be in your life and environment to close the Gap and ensure that this trajectory problem does not occur again.

To drill down for powerful Options, consider every letter within the Player Capability Index from within yourself, others, and even from your FIST Factor to ensure quality and quantity of contributions. If done thoroughly and effectively you should have volumes of foresight amass and limited after-the-fact hindsight flashes.

4. **P = Pick and Proceed.** Now evaluate from the above options which is most viable, based upon time allocations, financial abilities, and available resources. Be aware that you will always have multiple backup or contingency plans that you can draw upon should your first option not provide you the trajectory deliverables you need. Pick that option and proceed with complete commitment to address the Gap and get back onto trajectory pathway Point C.

5. **S = Start the process over.** Once you've deployed an action plan, always revisit and monitor your new decisions and trajectory to learn from them. This is the only way you'll ensure that you are in fact accomplishing what the Gap demands and what you desire. Make calculated calibrations or recalibrations as you proceed.

The simplicity yet comprehensiveness of the STOPS model allows you to independently or interactively facilitate the decision process to generate a final output and attain higher levels of trajectory success.

Bridging the Gap demands that you follow a game plan and possess the savvy ability to build alliances and attract key stakeholders to your cause. Consider Rule 80-10-10 in doing so. When initially engaging any group dynamic, and all things being equal at the outset, the demographic tends to break down into three distinctive subgroups. I identify the three subgroups as:

1. 80 = The first subgroup is the 80 percent we refer to as the followers. I visualize them at any given time as the "?" (question mark) people. There is nothing particularly positive or negative about them. At times you or I may be a follower; we really do not care what is done or how, and we will support whatever others wish to do. These become the foot soldiers for your goals, and you need as many as is appropriate for every trajectory. Look for people with similar IP Statements, and shared FIST Factor references as valuable and loyal followers.

2. 10 = The second subgroup is the 10 percent who are part of the influencer groups that you want to enlist to your cause in closing the Gap. This subgroup are the transformers or "+" people. You want to make sure they participate in the STOPS model process throughout, but at the very least the P step. This way, you'll know that you have their commitment and support when you launch your new trajectory. Their early buy-in and vocal support will attract the 80 percent to participate in your trajectory. Often, it can even completely shut down the third subgroup of distracters. But if the third subgroup senses you are solo, then they will derail you, either aggressively or passively. You can identify potential transformers from the total group by recognizing who among members of your FIST Factor have influence among others. They may have a specific vested interest in your new trajectory or are people with whom you have a personal connection (friends, people that like you, that you like, or who owe you a favor). Look for people with similar IP Statements and shared FIST Factor references as valuable and loyal transformers.

3. 10 = The third subgroup is the 10 percent who are part of one of the influencer groups that you want to manage, be mindful of, and work to eliminate or convert. Members of this

group typically speak first, fastest, and loudest—especially when they hear something that challenges their status quo or creates change, whether they understand it or not. These are the people you should designate with a "–" symbol. To begin to engage them, you always have to connect with the transformers first and the followers second, to ensure they are aligned with you and working to close the Gap. Then look for ways to begin to connect in a meaningful way with this last group in an effort to convert them to followers and eventually into active forward trajectory contributing transformers. You can do this by looking hard at some degree of similar IP Statement threads, potentially some similar shared FIST Factor references, or Player Capability Index references.

Bridging the Gap requires that you simultaneously explore the immediate, intermediate, and long-term congruency drivers that will allow your trajectory to proceed from Point B, where you are, to Point C, where you need to be. Remember that change is usually not an experience that people welcome with open arms. Ensure that other people understand and appreciate the need for change calibration and recalibration thoroughly, and that you have the support mechanisms and people in place to ensure forward movement. You may face some challenging times ahead, but maintaining focus on the ultimate trajectory goal will keep everyone on course.

---

### Redo You—The Line: *Your Trajectory Code*™ Calibrators/Windshield Application Time:

In order to manage your Line and ensure your trajectory growth and development, you as the reader must assume ownership of the calibrations that take place. You must address any issues that influence your personal trajectory growth, peer-to-peer interactions, or hinder your Line, and assume ownership of your professional organizational

*(continued)*

(*continued*)

trajectory advancement. Answer the following three questions to give you perspective on where you are on your Line.

**1.** Personal (Positional) Growth: Where are you now at Point A? Where are you on your Line based upon what you are doing? Is your trajectory headed toward Point B or Point C? What specific actions must you implement in the next 7/30/60 days to ensure your vocational positional trajectory pathway aims toward Point C?

_____

_____

**2.** Peer-to-Peer Influence Accountability: Where are you now? What is Point A? How are Lines intersecting based upon what you are doing and how others are interacting with you? Is your trajectory headed toward Point B or Point C? What specific actions must you implement in the next 7/30/60 days with a Peer Accountability Partner to ensure your trajectory pathway aims toward Point C?

_____

_____

**3.** Organizational Growth: Where are you now? What is Point A? Based on what you are doing, is your trajectory headed toward Point B or Point C? What specific actions must you implement in the next 7/30/60 days to ensure that your trajectory pathway within your organization moves you toward Point C needs?

_____

_____

*Trajectory Calibration*

# CHAPTER 9

# What Line Really Matters? Smart versus Safe Trajectory Decisions

The trajectory of a smart decision versus a safe decision is light years apart—and the incremental influences of each of these trajectories are significant, comprising the mental imprint of your TC and that of others. In a business, the difference can mean the influence on making market leaders or market followers. A manager makes safe decisions, and a leader makes smart decisions that, when extrapolated, can take you to Point B trajectory placements. Often, safe decisions are what lead to Gap implosions and bring you to an undesirable point.

Exploring why individuals may engage in a trajectory that involves safe versus smart decisions and actions can vary. But the following 10 items are some of the typical imprints for why you and others may select a less fulfilling Line in the end. We make safe decisions because:

1. We lack self-discipline when seeking trajectory perfection.
2. Stakeholders lack a sense of proactiveness; they're always waiting for someone else to make the decisions, or direct them to the implementation of a decision.
3. We lack independent thought capacity, which someone who really does lack the independent PCI depth to make a smart decision is typically aware of. This person works hard to deflect attention away from how bad they suc while castigating others. Subsequently, they constantly make safe decisions, regardless of intermediate or long-term trajectory needs—or whether in the end they arrive at Point B.
4. We don't have past or present culture dynamics that champion trajectory for smart and successful decisions. We can see evidence of this via policies, procedures, unions, litigation, lack of leadership skills, and other factors that foster safe decision trajectory.
5. We operate within a culture that champions and rewards being a follower and not a transformer.

6. We work in environments that tolerate or even reward passive-aggressive behaviors—meaning that others are conditioned to assume that someone will always enable them and cover for them.

7. Stakeholders that should be change agents and smart executioners are too concerned about what management thinks to take the risks necessary to set themselves on a winning trajectory.

8. Defensive posturing among individuals that otherwise wish to make and execute smart decisions have become so worn down that they no longer care to excel; they're just looking to get by.

9. That is all that is expected.

10. The culture in which one lives and works drives that behavior.

I once had a client who introduced me to a prospect of national prominence and spent hours telling me about the complete dearth of managerial-leadership-executive development programming in their organization. The lack of human capital talent and skilled ability they were experiencing in their C-Suite wasn't even coming close to meeting their CEO's expanding needs. But instead of opting for the obvious solution—a turnkey 24/7 year-long sequential psychological managerial-leadership series with multiple reinforcement and sustainment resources—they decided to go with the safe decision. They brought in a seminar series from a national name brand vendor (not even the innovator of the content; a mere trained talking-head!) that only addressed variables of need within the management ranks. They addressed a symptom and avoided the pain points, because it was safe and easy, not smart and necessary. Six months later everyone felt warm, fuzzy, and better. But no sequential psychological managerial-leadership-executive development was undertaken, and no one had delivered any solutions to the CEO.

Safe decisions may keep you under the radar of attention. However, the smart, bold (not reckless) decisions move your trajectory toward Point C destinations. But it requires you to have a sound TC, solid FIST Factor representation, clear IP Statement, and the ability to execute meaningfully at every opportunity that will allow you to be smart and not just safe.

Exploring why individuals may engage in a trajectory that involves smart decisions and actions versus safe decisions and actions can vary. Here are eight of the typical imprints that drive smart-decision trajectory:

1. Smart means intellectually informed, so that your PCI is engaged.
2. Smart means based upon fact, void of personal alliances or nepotism.
3. Smart means your IP Statement is driving your TC and a personal code-of-ethics that you will never have to explain or justify.
4. Smart means the decisions, based upon all available evidence and facts, will always be on the same trajectory. It's like telling the truth in that you never have to remember what you said last time because it will always be the same next time.
5. Smart means your FIST Factor is balanced, engaged, and challenging your trajectory decisions in an objective manner.
6. Smart means your decisions adhere to the STOPS model.
7. Smart decisions follow the trajectory for the immediate, intermediate, and long term (as best as you can forecast long-term at this Point A). These decisions are integral and aligned to get you to Point C and need to be void of personal favoritisms, personal vested self-interest, or the enrichment of others at the ultimate Point C.
8. You make smart decisions because the culture in which you live and work encourages that behavior.

The challenge is to not be making long-term decisions based upon short-term needs. This almost always ensures that you derail off of the intended trajectory pathways. It is critical to be able to mentally play forward every action, every inner dialogue imprint, reference the TC assets you now have (a sound FIST Factor, greater awareness of your PCI depth and opportunities for growth, a retooled IP Statement, etc.), and ensure that trajectory is what consumes your energies.

---

### Redo You—The Line: *Your Trajectory Code*™ Calibrators/Windshield Application Time:

In order to manage your Line and ensure your trajectory growth and development, you as the reader must assume ownership of the calibrations that take place. You must address any issues that influence your personal trajectory growth, peer-to-peer interactions, or hinder your Line, and assume ownership of your professional organizational trajectory advancement. Answer the following three questions to give you perspective on where you are on your Line.

**1.** Personal (Positional) Growth: Where are you now at Point A? Where are you on your Line based upon what you are doing? Is your trajectory headed toward Point B or Point C? What specific actions must you implement in the next 7/30/60 days to ensure your vocational positional trajectory pathway aims toward Point C?

_____

_____

_____

_____

**2.** Peer-to-Peer Influence Accountability: Where are you now? What is Point A? How are Lines intersecting based upon what you are doing and how others are interacting with you? Is your trajectory headed toward Point B or Point C? What specific actions must you implement in the next 7/30/60 days with a Peer Accountability Partner to ensure your trajectory pathway aims toward Point C?

_____

_____

_____

_____

**3.** Organizational Growth: Where are you now? What is Point A? Based on what you are doing, is your trajectory headed toward Point B or Point C? What specific actions must you implement in the next

7/30/60 days to ensure that your trajectory pathway within your
organization moves you toward Point C needs?

_____

_____

_____

_____

Trajectory Calibration

# CHAPTER 10

# Intersecting Lines

## *Thinking about Lateral and Vertical Trajectories*

The pathways you cross will inevitably influence your ultimate trajectory experiences and end-points. The more you can think ahead and recognize the trajectories of those around you—both laterally and vertically—the better you'll be able to forecast ways to collaborate and succeed with others. This can also help you recognize possible trajectory collision points and keep them from throwing you off-course.

Thinking in lateral trajectory terms requires you to reflect on how your trajectory may influence and impact those on your same lateral level, and how others can help or hinder your trajectory. You must attempt to recognize what you know about others' IP Statements and the depth of their PCI as you engage with them. This will help you determine how to leverage and complement one another, and do so without provoking any negative energy from others.

Thinking in lateral trajectory terms requires asking how you engage different constituents, such as your:

- Peers
- Colleagues
- Equals
- Circle-of-Influence
- Pay Grade Equivalents
- Individuals with similar certification qualifiers, rank, titles, tenure, etc.
- Others as trajectories make apparent

By recognizing you do not live in a vacuum, your ability to engage others and not project a self-absorbed image will aid you greatly in soliciting support and assisting others in reaching their trajectory Point C goals. Remember that there may be competitive trajectories from time to time with others on a lateral level; these can be very tricky maneuverings for you. As the saying goes, "Be careful of what bridges you burn, as you may need to come back across them one day."

Point C is about championship, success, victories, and achievement. The more you can help others get to this place, the more *you* will experience your Point C trajectory pathways. This will help you focus on staying on trajectory for the long-term Points, as most people around you will not be operating from the TC matrix or balance.

Reflect upon your peer group at this stage. Think about the organizations for which you work, volunteer, and associate. Recognize the IP Statements of colleagues and how they showcase them daily to you and others. Recognize what their PCI depth is as you meet them and as your careers develop. Recognize the people with whom they associate and assimilate via their FIST Factor. Remember, it is both guilt by association *and* success by association. As your career pathway trajectory moves you forward, and in observing or working with others with similarly shaped TCs, recognize how each new calibration shapes your own TC. Consider:

- The depth of others' PCI. How can you help them—and how can they help you—to grow and attain one another's Point Cs from an immediate, intermediate, and long-term perspective?
- Recognize how others manage their own trajectories. How do their actions impact their trajectory pathways toward Point B or Point C? What lessons can you learn from them?
- How do others reveal or not reveal their IP Statements in an attempt to manage their trajectory pathway toward Point C?
- How do you stay connected with individuals of high stock value as both their and your career trajectories progress?
- Recognize how others' value line within the PFC FISHES model influences their efforts, commitments, and trajectory. Can the associated costs or benefits of those efforts provide either a positive or negative benchmark for you?

- Explore how you can blend your trajectories with others' so you both can attain greater trajectory successes.

Thinking in a vertical trajectory way compels you to consider how your trajectory may influence and impact those senior to or above you in any matrix hierarchy. It will prompt thoughts of how those individuals can outwardly or privately help or hinder your trajectory. How can you help make other people look good and be an asset for them? How do you do so without provoking any negative energies or appearing high-maintenance?

Thinking in terms of vertical trajectory means asking how you can respect, support, and engage different constituents, such as:

- Supervisors and their supervisors
- Anyone who sees themselves as a boss to you
- Individuals of reverence
- Anyone that you see as upward on any ladder-of-life area you serve and work within
- Individuals of influence in your personal or professional life trajectories
- Individuals of greater pay grade
- Individuals with greater certification qualifiers, rank, titles, tenure, etc.
- Generationally your elders
- Others as trajectories make apparent

As your trajectory takes you across others' lateral and vertical trajectories, always be mindful of how you negotiate that intersection, and how it appears through the eyes of others. If others see you as a complement and a strategic asset that can provide value unlike anyone else at that moment in time, then they're likely to overlook any minor gaffes and gaps. You'll develop a reputation as an individual who has other people's best interests in mind. Your trajectory pathways will seldom be interrupted or derailed.

Consider the same matters from a vertical perspective that you did from a lateral:

- The depth of others' PCI. How can you help them—and how can they help you—to grow and attain one another's Point Cs from an immediate, intermediate, and long-term perspective?
- Recognize how others manage their own trajectories. How do their actions impact their trajectory pathway toward Point B or Point C? What lessons can you learn from them?
- How do others reveal or not reveal their IP Statements in an attempt to manage their trajectory pathways toward Point C?
- How do you stay connected with individuals of high stock value as both their and your career trajectories progress?
- Recognize how others' value line within the PFC FISHES model influences their efforts, commitments, and trajectory. Can the associated costs or benefits of those efforts provide either a positive or negative benchmark for you?
- Explore how you can blend your trajectories with others' so you both can attain greater trajectory successes.

Recognize your trajectory and the pathways you cross en route to your Point C destinations, as they will have an influence on your ultimate trajectory experiences and end-points. The more you can think ahead of your own trajectory and recognize the trajectories of those around you, both laterally and vertically, the more you can forecast ways to collaborate and succeed with others.

---

### Redo You—The Line: *Your Trajectory Code*™ Calibrators/Windshield Application Time:

In order to manage your Line and ensure your trajectory growth and development, you as the reader must assume ownership of the calibrations that take place. You must address any issues that influence your personal trajectory growth, peer-to-peer interactions, or hinder your Line, and assume ownership of your professional organizational trajectory advancement. Answer the following three questions to give you perspective on where you are on your Line.

1. **Personal (Positional) Growth:** Where are you now at Point A? Where are you on your Line based upon what you are doing? Is your trajectory headed toward Point B or Point C? What specific actions must you implement in the next 7/30/60 days to ensure your vocational positional trajectory pathway aims toward Point C?

   _____

   _____

   _____

2. **Peer-to-Peer Influence Accountability:** Where are you now? What is Point A? How are Lines intersecting based upon what you are doing and how others are interacting with you? Is your trajectory headed toward Point B or Point C? What specific actions must you implement in the next 7/30/60 days with a Peer Accountability Partner to ensure your trajectory pathway aims toward Point C?

   _____

   _____

   _____

3. **Organizational Growth:** Where are you now? What is Point A? Based on what you are doing, is your trajectory headed toward Point B or Point C? What specific actions must you implement in the next 7/30/60 days to ensure that your trajectory pathway within your organization moves you toward Point C needs?

   _____

   _____

   _____

   _____

_Trajectory Calibration_

# CHAPTER 11

# The Cracks in the Line

## *Relationships Can Make or Break Your Trajectories*

Your ultimate trajectory acceleration and ability to attain Point C destinations will always depend upon your ability to craft meaningful interactions or relationships with others. Failing to do so can derail your trajectory or, even worse, lead to dominant negative inner dialogues in your head. Moreover, this feeds destructive FIST Factors, decaying IP Statements, and a shallow depth of PCI factors. Relationships must be built upon substance for their value to grow.

Situational relationships may serve an immediate need and trajectory, but they will not hold firm and sustain intermediate and long-term needs. Crises may arise that will bring together people who would not otherwise have been likely to intersect pathways. But unless someone leverages this chance trajectory interaction to forge deeper connections, these too will be fleeting at best. Once lost, relationships are hard to ever be regained and constructively utilized. However, healthy relationships can be sustained over time, even if the participants are not connected throughout the entire period of time.

Your TC will influence the relationships you have, how you value each, and the trajectories you take within each. Your IP Statement will also determine who you're open to meeting and forging relationships with, as well as those you may never notice because you do not make yourself available.

It's also necessary to self-reflect and run a tough diagnostic on the FIST Factor you started with in this book. This will help you recognize whether it has evolved through the pages into a larger, more profound, and robustly diverse healthy FIST Factor of imprints upon you. Do you bring unhealthy relationships (people from your past trajectories that are not reflective of your future trajectory) with you into these pages? Has their influence held you back from actualizing greatness? Do they continuously feed your TC with false imprints that are damaging to you and to potential great relationships with others?

Sometimes to evolve forward toward long-term Point C trajectories, we must transition our immediate and intermediate trajectory away from past calibration influences. In more than two decades of work with more than 2 million individuals from all walks of life, it has become evident to me that all sustained healthy relationships consist of a minimum of four core ingredients, factors, or elements.

So, what is the architecture of a healthy, balanced relationship that can be sustained by your TC? Consider as a visual reference point the Relationship Cube™ in Figure 11.1, which has four sides upon which to base relationships. With each side defined and continuously reinforced, individuals can forge interactive, healthy relationships. The work comes in understanding what the meaningful support calibrators to each side are for each person with whom you engage.

Imagine the Relationship Cube as a bank account held between you and the other person(s). There are four ways to make a deposit into the account. Your objective is to learn what kind of deposits are meaningful for the other person, to always be mindful of that, and make only that kind of deposit. The deposits are the currency to the relationship and will provide greater success in your trajectory goals in life. Not knowing what the deposits are—or making the incorrect kind—can lead to a relationship implosion in the future, much like no longer having an overdraft protection clause in the account with the other person(s).

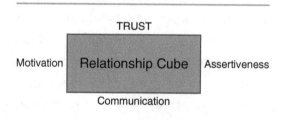

**FIGURE 11.1   Relationship Cube**

The strength of a relationship is predicated upon the type and amount of deposits you have made to or withdrawals you have made from the account. The more you understand about what they appreciate or desire, the greater your insight into value calibrators. The more your deposits have value to the other person(s), the greater your relationships will become. The greater the relationships are, the greater your connections become to enrich your TC, your FIST Factors, and your IP Statement.

Table 11.1 is merely a beginning template of what I have found to be some of the universal deposits into each side of the Relationship Cube account.

If the Relationship Cube account was all about you, what other individual deposits would need to appear under each side category to have value meaning for you? Are there any calibrator deposits in Table 11.1 that, if presented, would not really be meaningful to or from you or others? This recognition of your own preferences is critical for gasping this overall concept. It will either have a constructive or counterproductive influence upon your ability to achieve trajectory Point C in life.

Having healthy relationships with people in each level of your PFS FISHES model and within your trajectory pathways can

## TABLE 11.1  Relationship Cube Matrix

| Deposits | TRUST | Assertiveness | Motivation | Communication |
|----------|-------|---------------|------------|---------------|
| | Honesty | Allow Opinions | Thank You | Listen |
| | Empower | Empower | Empower | Empower |
| | Integrity | Give Ownership | Rewards | Ask Questions |
| | Confidence | Delegate | Awards | Feedback |
| | Support | Support | Support | Support |
| | Be A Leader | Make Them Safe | Compensation | Share Info |
| | Defend Me | Stand Up To Others | Promote Me | Talk |
| | Do What You Say | Freedom | Praise | Take Notes |

either expedite or hinder your success. Knowing and letting others know what your deposits are is critical, as is knowing about others' deposits, and providing assistance that helps fill their needs. And interestingly enough, it's frequently the people that you do not initially notice who may well play a role in your trajectory now and in the future. This is why it's so crucial to be mindful of everyone in both lateral and vertical pathways.

To manage these relationships, recognize that you may extend overdraft protection to those you like and in whom you have a direct vested interest. It may also happen that these very people may become your most self-destructive forces, members of your FIST Factor, and trajectory derailers. You must be able to recognize when a relationship trajectory is entering into a bad credit or toxic direction and shut that account down. Closing an account can be the hardest immediate trajectory act you will experience; yet the intermediate and long-term effects of doing so will become the most rewarding. At these recalibrations, it is critical that you have done the early work detailed in this book and have retooled your IP Statement. This will serve you well in knowing when it is time to adjust your relationship accounts and retool the makeup of your FIST Factor.

Likewise, recognize that sometimes these Relationship Cube trajectory adjustments will require you to do some work on yourself. It might not be the other person(s) that is making incorrect deposits and has reached overdraft protection problems. If you're the one out of balance, you need to work on yourself to restore the relationship.

Your ultimate trajectory acceleration and ability to attain Point C destinations depends entirely on whether you can connect meaningfully with others. You must also recognize when a relationship has lived its natural lifecycle and is becoming, or has become, unhealthy. If you can't facilitate a beneficial intervention with the other party to communicate the deposit needs, then it is time to separate and move your trajectory onward.

---

### Redo You—The Line: *Your Trajectory Code*™ Calibrators/Windshield Application Time:

In order to manage your Line and ensure your trajectory growth and development, you as the reader must assume ownership of the calibrations that take place. You must address any issues that influence your personal trajectory growth, peer-to-peer interactions, or hinder your Line, and assume ownership of your professional organizational trajectory advancement. Answer the following three questions to give you perspective on where you are on your Line.

1. Personal (Positional) Growth: Where are you now at Point A? Where are you on your Line based upon what you are doing? Is your trajectory headed toward Point B or Point C? What specific actions must you implement in the next 7/30/60 days to ensure your vocational positional trajectory pathway aims toward Point C?

   _____

   _____

   _____

   _____

   _____

2. Peer-to-Peer Influence Accountability: Where are you now? What is Point A? How are Lines intersecting based upon what you are doing and how others are interacting with you? Is your trajectory headed toward Point B or Point C? What specific actions must you implement in the next 7/30/60 days with a Peer Accountability Partner to ensure your trajectory pathway aims toward Point C?

   _____

   _____

   _____

   _____

3. Organizational Growth: Where are you now? What is Point A? Based on what you are doing, is your trajectory headed toward Point B or Point C? What specific actions must you implement

*(continued)*

(continued)

in the next 7/30/60 days to ensure that your trajectory pathway within your organization moves you toward Point C needs?

_____

_____

_____

_____

_____

Trajectory Calibration

# CHAPTER 12

# Alignment

## *Blending Trajectories with Others for Shared Success*

Alignment of your trajectory with others' is a critical thing to understand, as this will allow for accelerated ROI (return on investments) of energy, endeavor, and ultimate results. Proper alignments provide immediate, intermediate, and long-term calibration clues as to when you are on Pathway" and when you may, at a very early stage of evolving, have moved off-track and onto Pathway B, or what we have identified as the 1 percent factors.

Blending your trajectories with those of the others does not need to mean that you are making concessions or letting the other party win. This process simply encourages you to find acceptable or even better alternatives to getting from Point A to Point C in the most efficient manner possible. And when you can do so in a way to accommodate and aid others, even better.

Many times an ineffective TC programmed for yesterday hinders your effectiveness for now and the future. This, compounded by an unhealthy FIST Factor, a decaying and outdated IP Statement, or a clouded rearview focus, can cause one to see blending trajectories as a bad idea. We see this in organizational politics far too often. If a leader makes it safe for those around you to share even unpopular information, or challenge ideas, then you break through the politics. If you strive to apply the Player Capability Index to what you do and how you task or elevate those around you, then the politics of favoritism will be diminished by the realities of capability. In these situations, the ability to strive toward and exceed trajectory Point C will be a common experience and reality. It takes a leader to break out of this downward, inward, self-destructive trajectory, always destined for Point B.

So how do you calibrate your trajectory to be able to blend with others for common gains? Start by:

- Looking for shared entry points where you and the other party may see you have something in common.
- Learning what the other person's IP Statement is. Then use this to gauge mutual beliefs and values to uncover common

pathway points between Point A and Point C that you can travel together.

Becoming fixated upon a particular pathway to Point C can deter you, as it may be just one of many acceptable action plans that a neutral third party sees. So step back and recognize what has caused you to reach an impasse with others. Try to see your pathway through the lens of another person.

Blending with others requires you to keep an eye open for opportunities to assist and align with them. People can be hesitant to allow others to help them. But when individuals see you as a conduit to their success and someone who can aid them, then they tend to be less defensive.

It's critical to think about how we present ourselves to others and how they hear us. American motivational teacher and speaker Zig Ziglar was fond of saying that when we listen to others, we listen to them as if we were listening to a radio station. All radio stations have call letters and therefore, the number one radio station frequency through which we all listen in our head is WIIFM—that is, What's In It For Me (WIIFM). If the signal plays correctly, we take action and if not, we tune out.

So to motivate individuals to consider our blended trajectories, we must get groups of people to come together for ultimate universal Point C destinations. In these situations, play your proposition over a second radio-station metaphor, WIIFU—What's In It For Us!

Blending trajectory pathways is about finding acceptable or even better alternatives for getting from Point A to Point C in the most efficient manner possible—and when you can do so in a way that accommodates others, even better. Some strategies for this approach include:

- Engaging one-on-one with the other key stakeholder(s) and highlighting PCI strengths to determine how they can be leveraged for greater Point C gains. This will help you uncover how to combine your strengths to complement one another for even greater gains.

- Enlist the buy-in and support of transformers (matriarchs and patriarchs to a given situation, cause, group) for alignment of energies to ensure no rogue players implode trajectories, once put into motion.
- Play to a higher cause. Sometimes there may be a greater Point C on the other person's trajectory goal. Your ability to identify it may provide you a perspective on ways to engage them and gain their support in a shared trajectory.

I once worked with a national volunteer organization that elects their president annually. Their membership is generationally termed out, making the potential for politics and ego great. They would have a better chance of getting the current president to recognize they had 12 months to reign if they could identify specific Point C goals and enlist the ownership of the elder board members by merging the best ideas. Then the majority of the followers (members) would embrace it and the level of Point C success would be amazing. Once they did this, the results were in fact amazing. By getting the president to realize that within that organization there was nowhere upward to go, their entire legacy focused on what they accomplished with and through others, and made a mental shift from trajectory Point B tradition to trajectory Point C future-based reality.

Sometimes merging your energies with others can provide a greater synergy and potential positive outcome. When you can eliminate duplication of effort systems, and engage processes to eliminate redundancies, you can actually accelerate your trajectory calibration and Point C arrival.

One way to motivate yourself or the other party to blend trajectories is simply to ask what the level of pain factor or pleasure factor would be for various activities. Psychology teaches us that we act or change our behavior based upon a perceived level of pain or pleasure. If either pain is lacking or pleasure is extreme, a person will continue with their actions and behavior. So consider the level and extremes of pain or pleasure that can be unleashed in various scenarios. For example, is the pain of admitting weakness or lack of expertise in a particular area worth the pleasure of getting a project right the first time? Yes, probably.

If you see that adopting or blending with another's trajectory will make your life better (pleasure) then you will typically be very willing to blend and less likely to resist others' trajectories. Conversely, if you see that your life will become worse by doing so, you aren't as likely to accept or embrace others' trajectories.

Referring back to Figure I.1, you'll notice the arrows between Points B and C at the top of the diagram. The line pointing from Point C toward Point B is not about blending; rather, it indicates abandoning the trajectory that is healthy in the immediate, intermediate, and long term, to accommodate the individual(s) at Point B. This move will always lead to continued problems. This is where an enabled and entitlement orientation is created within a person's TC and where the degradation, degeneration, and divisiveness mentality comes from.

The bridge, if you will, from Point B to Point C is essential to getting back on track. Your values drive your vision, which in turn propels your operating mission statements to Point C. When you have these aligned within yourself and with the people with whom you interact with or serve, you're much less likely to experience degradation of your TC.

Many times the trajectory lines are moved from the wrong side inward to appease a vocal minority that has never been held accountable. These times of attempted blending likely require others to retool their IP Statements, FIST Factors, mental Teeter-Totters, and to realign their PFC FISHES matrix. Everything is out of balance and a major recalibration is necessary for them to ever begin to recognize that blending trajectories would yield greater dividends for them and anyone they may care about around them.

When the trajectory Point B line moves as the arrow indicates toward Point C, in either 1 percent factors or significant trajectory recalibration efforts, it does not need to mean that you are making trajectory concessions by blending your trajectories with those of others. It means that you're finding different, or even better, faster, more cost-efficient alternatives for getting from Point A to Point C.

---

### Redo You—The Line: *Your Trajectory Code*™ Calibrators/Windshield Application Time:

In order to manage your Line and ensure your trajectory growth and development, you as the reader must assume ownership of the calibrations that take place. You must address any issues that influence your personal trajectory growth, peer-to-peer interactions, or hinder your Line, and assume ownership of your professional organizational trajectory advancement. Answer the following three questions to give you perspective on where you are on your Line.

1. Personal (Positional) Growth: Where are you now at Point A? Where are you on your Line based upon what you are doing? Is your trajectory headed toward Point B or Point C? What specific actions must you implement in the next 7/30/60 days to ensure your vocational positional trajectory pathway aims toward Point C?

   _____

   _____

   _____

   _____

2. Peer-to-Peer Influence Accountability: Where are you now? What is Point A? How are Lines intersecting based upon what you are doing and how others are interacting with you? Is your trajectory headed toward Point B or Point C? What specific actions must you implement in the next 7/30/60 days with a Peer Accountability Partner to ensure your trajectory pathway aims toward Point C?

   _____

   _____

   _____

   _____

*(continued)*

*(continued)*

**3.** Organizational Growth: Where are you now? What is Point A? Based on what you are doing, is your trajectory headed toward Point B or Point C? What specific actions must you implement in the next 7/30/60 days to ensure that your trajectory pathway within your organization moves you toward Point C needs?

_____

_____

_____

_____

*Trajectory Calibration*

CHAPTER **13**

# The Power of
# Low Expectations

This chapter title may have caused you to scratch your head a bit. However, this doesn't mean setting the trajectory line low as a strategy to set someone up for success. Rather, it addresses the damaging degradation of returns on investment from allowing the performance bar to be set low and celebrated.

In the face of demoralizing energy, being penalized for achieving trajectory greatness, or recognizing that those around you are being rewarded for minimal accomplishments, people will begin to recalibrate their performance trajectory downward. When individuals realize they can reduce their output and benefit at the same time, it can become human nature to calibrate downward their participation and behavior while getting the big rewards. When individuals and groups create a trajectory of high expectations and low participation, this becomes manifested when no one holds them accountable but the payoffs keep coming. If the payoff for minimal performance is granted or, even worse, if payoffs are awarded for low to no performance, that performance will be repeated.

Once this takes root, the power of low expectations sets in. You start looking for statistical data to actually support reasons for the downward trajectory as both acceptable and not the fault or responsibility of the low performers. Then you will recognize that the lack of personal accountability feeds this trend, which then becomes an addiction that drives the key influencers around it.

A simple application of the Player Capability Index can reveal the shortcomings that have allowed this behavior to occur. However, each letter within the Player Capability Index formula also uncovers opportunities for deflection away from oneself and one's weaknesses. It does damage in the long run, since lowering of the performance bar begins to shape people's Trajectory Code to be average. The power of low expectations can kill entrepreneurial energy and drive the mental DNA downward to the place where the blind lead the blind.

Personal immediate accountability and having accountability mechanisms in place are critical to detecting trajectory behavior that leads to pathway B early on, so that simple 1 percent factors can be administered to recalibrate to pathway C destinations.

---

### Redo You—The Line: *Your Trajectory Code*™ Calibrators/Windshield Application Time:

In order to manage your Line and ensure your trajectory growth and development, you as the reader must assume ownership of the calibrations that take place. You must address any issues that influence your personal trajectory growth, peer-to-peer interactions, or hinder your Line, and assume ownership of your professional organizational trajectory advancement. Answer the following three questions to give you perspective on where you are on your Line.

1. Personal (Positional) Growth: Where are you now at Point A? Where are you on your Line based upon what you are doing? Is your trajectory headed toward Point B or Point C? What specific actions must you implement in the next 7/30/60 days to ensure your vocational positional trajectory pathway aims toward Point C?

    _____

    _____

    _____

    _____

2. Peer-to-Peer Influence Accountability: Where are you now? What is Point A? How are Lines intersecting based upon what you are doing and how others are interacting with you? Is your trajectory headed toward Point B or Point C? What specific actions must you implement in the next 7/30/60 days with a Peer Accountability Partner to ensure your trajectory pathway aims toward Point C?

    _____

    _____

    _____

3. Organizational Growth: Where are you now? What is Point A? Based on what you are doing, is your trajectory headed toward Point B or Point C? What specific actions must you implement

in the next 7/30/60 days to ensure that your trajectory pathway within your organization moves you toward Point C needs?

_____

_____

_____

_____

_____

Trajectory Calibration

# CHAPTER 14

# Purposeful You and Your Trajectory Code

## *Victim or Victor? Your Self-Talk Is Critical*

You can the view Trajectory Calibration diagram (see Figure I.1) as a "V" for Victory or as another mental reference imprint—a Victim sign. With a better understanding of your historical Trajectory Code imprints, you can now take ownership to maintain your trajectory pathway. Similarly, you can calibrate your TC with new imprints and change from Pathway B to an ever-successful Pathway C, for the immediate, intermediate, and long-term destiny.

You can recognize how every immediate action and decision can have constructive positive implications on subsequent decisions and actions. Conversely, you can also recognize from your TC how an immediate, irrational, emotion-based action or decision can have lasting negative consequences and ramifications upon your pathways.

As Dr. Bill Cosby and Dr. Alvin Poussaint detailed in their classic book, *Come on, People: On the Path from Victims to Victors*, the things that hold us back from greatest pathway successes in life are not the outward stimulants one would like to blame, but often things within us. So, to better navigate toward victory for oneself, within an organization, or society, it is critical to understand other players' TCs. You cannot change a past trajectory pathway, but you can—and must—alter the future.

Many people go through life having allowed their emotional windshield to take over. They become so headstrong in their actions that they make no observations and allow themselves no permission to acknowledge poor trajectory decisions or make necessary recalibrations. At this point, they and everyone else ends up at Point B, where the challenge to change is so great that it becomes paralyzing. So instead of making any alterations, people defer back to almost primal behaviors—like blaming others and acting the victim.

Understanding both your own and others' imprints and TC can help you forecast whether victory or victimhood is in your or their future. It can help determine whether you will be an active imprint participant in that victory or will be played into victimhood. Ask the questions behind the questions to unveil deep-seated imprint beliefs of others that drive their pathway actions—questions like:

- How do they chronicle their early-year trajectory influencers and imprints?
- What were their formal and informal childhood environments like? What expectations were placed upon them in both?
- Who were their childhood and adolescent influencers, mentors, guides, and activities?
- Were they an active leader, participant, or follower? Of what groups, associations, activities, belief shapers, and so on?
- Where did they live geographically or travel growing up? Do any of these places bring unique additional imprints (refer to all above questions) upon them?
- When did they leave any degree of safety or family environment to be on their own trajectory in life from their solo decisions?
- Where did they receive any education in life that shaped their imprints for present pathway actions?
- Explore their private sector employment, nonprofit employment, or welfare recipient positioning.
- What are their political or religious views? Though this is sensitive territory, these elements almost always play a part in early-life imprinting.

Continue to ask these questions behind the questions as you evaluate yourself and others. They will naturally lead to a new set of questions that give you ever better clarity.

You can evaluate organizations the same way—by identifying the real fundamental leaders and shapers of the organization. Their TC imprint typically influences whatever the organization posts as their TC—otherwise known as the values, core beliefs, core competencies sought, and ultimate mission statement.

Whether to move yourself toward victory in the presence of others, or to participate within an organization and attain victory, the same pathway is required. Understand the TC imprints that have shaped and directed the trajectory up to that point. If that information gives you a blueprint for continued engagement for Point C success, then move forward. If information gives you the understanding that you or the organization may implode, then begin the work of introducing new imprints and reinforce those imprints with your every action.

Listen to your self-talk. Recognize your internal dialogue, whether it comes from a point of forward-focused, constructive windshield orientation or whether you're living in the past and engaging in self-defeating internal conversations. A forward focus will allow you to draw upon the strengths of your Player Capability Index. When you hear the constructive self-talk, celebrate it and allow it to manifest even greater solutions and opportunities. When you hear the negative self-talk, immediately shut it down and push that internal dialogue toward solutions, positive FIST Factor influences, and work for and toward balancing your trajectory pathways. Remember, one powerful way to recognize the trajectory pathway that you are on (Point B or Point C) is to simply listen to the internal dialogues you have. Guide both yourself and others toward their Point C by consistently and repeatedly working toward windshield time, every time you digress.

You can change your trajectory and you can change others' trajectory destination; it simply takes repeated, calm, and fact-based reinforcement.

---

### Redo You—The Line: *Your Trajectory Code™* Calibrators/Windshield Application Time:

In order to manage your Line and ensure your trajectory growth and development, you as the reader must assume ownership of the calibrations that take place. You must address any issues that influence your personal trajectory growth, peer-to-peer interactions, or hinder your Line, and assume ownership of your professional organizational

*(continued)*

(*continued*)

trajectory advancement. Answer the following three questions to give you perspective on where you are on your Line.

1. **Personal (Positional) Growth:** Where are you now at Point A? Where are you on your Line based upon what you are doing? Is your trajectory headed toward Point B or Point C? What specific actions must you implement in the next 7/30/60 days to ensure your vocational positional trajectory pathway aims toward Point C?

   _____

   _____

2. **Peer-to-Peer Influence Accountability:** Where are you now? What is Point A? How are Lines intersecting based upon what you are doing and how others are interacting with you? Is your trajectory headed toward Point B or Point C? What specific actions must you implement in the next 7/30/60 days with a Peer Accountability Partner to ensure your trajectory pathway aims toward Point C?

   _____

   _____

3. **Organizational Growth:** Where are you now? What is Point A? Based on what you are doing, is your trajectory headed toward Point B or Point C? What specific actions must you implement in the next 7/30/60 days to ensure that your trajectory pathway within your organization moves you toward Point C needs?

   _____

   _____

*Trajectory Calibration*

# CHAPTER 15

# Conclusion

## *Trajectory Do-Over and Core Driver*

The Mental DNA Imprint to Who You Are, What You Do, and How to Design an Adaptive Attitude for Achievement for Your Next Trajectory!

By this point, this text has equipped you with the tools to make you capable of:

- Examining your Trajectory Code (TC) for what it is—without judgment—and beginning to make making strategic conscious steps to build a more healthy and balanced TC.
- Examining your FIST Factor for what it is—without judgment—and beginning to make strategic conscious steps to build a healthy and balanced FIST Factor and micro FIST Factors for situational needs. Challenge these people to challenge you, to calibrate your actions and decisions for significantly better trajectory pathways in life and more Point C destinations.
- Examining your Identity-Purpose Statement as it serves as your personal GPS for both how you see yourself and how you calibrate or recalibrate your entire thought process. This directs your natural inner dialogue based on these two imprint variables and helps you recognize what percentage of time you spend in the rearview-mirror of life versus operating from the windshield.
- Recognizing that the single common denominator of great people is that they assume ownership of their trajectory and allow it to continuously energize them.
- Being relentless in playing to your X-Factor and guiding your trajectories accordingly.
- Examining your Player Capability Index for what it is—without judgment—and beginning to make strategic conscious decisions. You'll implement the tactical commitments to build a deeper, more diverse, and thorough mental DNA to provide real meaning and value to you, others, and the planet.

- Examining your balance through the **PFC FISHES** model and recognizing that you cannot derive balance from the amount of time you spend in each category. Rather, it comes from the degree of importance you give to each category and weighing that against the amount of time you invest there.
- Recognizing that there are shift drivers that can further accelerate your trajectory away from Point B and toward Point C—as well as shifters that can derail you—and acknowledging how critical it is to stay focused and bridge the Gap for even greater successes in life.
- Deciding not to settle for safe decisions when trajectories require smart decisions. Recognizing how to make smart decisions and empower others around you to do the same.
- Remaining mindful of the implications of your trajectory on the lateral and vertical influencers around you for your immediate, intermediate, and long-term needs.
- Translating the four cornerstone variables, Trust, Assertiveness, Motivation, and Communication, into effective interactions and building the Relationship Cube between you and others.
- Remembering that trajectory pathways will take you into interactions with others and will test your ability to blend. To facilitate blending among others will always allow for greater sustained Point C endings!

You have had the opportunity to mentally or physically calibrate your trajectory or recalibrate your trajectory at the end of each chapter with the three trajectory questions. It is therefore your job to determine what calibrations take place for personal trajectory growth, peer-to-peer interactions, and within your professional organizational trajectory advancement, development, and growth.

This applies to you on both a personal and professional level. This book will begin your journey, quest, and conversation along this trajectory pathway. However, it will by no means be the complete work you will undergo. You can share this book with those around you to accelerate their trajectory pathway successes in life as well.

Your motives, values, and psychological needs calibrate your trajectory on a daily basis. You design your Trajectory Code to accept or reject any signal consistent or inconsistent with its architecture.

If you remember only one GPS idea from this text, it is as simple as A-B-C:

- Point A is always the starting point and how your TC shapes your every action.
- Point B is the representation of where your actual behaviors, actions, and influences may be directing your trajectory.
- Point C is always the intended goal, target, and trajectory destination.

Understanding what constitutes your TC imprints will make these 1 percent recalibrations easy to undertake. You can meet them with minimal resistance—and they'll yield significantly different outcomes. Remember, you don't want to awaken at Point B and see Point C off in the distance. Be mindful of the 1 percent calibrators right now, and always extrapolate outward as to what destination that calibration action will take you. The amount of smart work necessary to get onto trajectory track C is not always significant; it simply requires remaining consistently aware of your trajectory.

Your Trajectory Code and Core Driver are now what—and who—you determine it to be. You are the single dominant driver to your TC, as it will determine your trajectory pathway and how far beyond Point B or Point C you will arrive!

## Bonus Trajectory Options ... Enhancing the Line!©

### *What's Next?*

To ensure your trajectory and the influencers to your TC allow you to excel within your X-Factor space and that you are continuously growing your PCI, consider adding these (and like calibrators) into your life:

1. Subscribe to every trajectory resource at www.JeffreyMagee.com.
2. Subscribe to every hardcopy edition or online edition of *PERFORMANCE/P360 Magazine* at www.ProfessionalPerformanceMagazine.com as a positive Trajectory resource.
3. Contact the author at drjeffspeaks@aol.com to find out about coaching, mentoring, and training courses specific for your Line and trajectory needs.
4. Make a date with yourself every week (one hour personal development time, at a minimum) and expose yourself to intellectual ideas that enrich your TC and allow you to remain focused through the windshield and not in the rearview-mirror.

   This could be a variety of things: committing to reading a nonfiction book in any need area of your life as directed by a gap or void in the PCI model; or subscribing to an online journal, article series, or blog from a true thought-leader; participating in a town-hall experience live or online; attending a conference, workshop, class, or meet-up group of like-minded people or subject-matter-experts (SMEs); subscribing or reading magazines, white papers, and textbooks for an academic side to your trajectory C needs; or stopping into YouTube or online TED Talks and exposing yourself to fast mental insights for increased success.
5. Notice what your Line really showcases about you. Be legitimate by belonging to every trade association appropriate

to your craft, and be an active intellectual consumer of the deliverables it provides (Player Capability Index enhancer time). Associate with only the best of the best windshield performers in that trade association and continuously work to elevate the performance bar of excellence of everyone around you within that organization. If there are earned credentials that the trade association provides, go for them, have them, and accelerate beyond them.

6. If you have a smartphone or digital calendar system, make an automatic notation once a week for the next 12 months to remind you to partake in various activities, such as:

  a. Read a nonfiction book (biography, autobiography, popular trade book, academic textbook) in your area of TC growth and trajectory pathway C development.

  b. Read a traditional or online digital magazine or journal in your area of TC growth and trajectory pathway C development.

  c. Spend time with your mentor or performance coach as an accountability check within your area of TC growth and trajectory pathway C development.

  d. Search, join, participate in a PFC FISHES association, support group, or activity in your area of TC growth and trajectory pathway C development.

  e. Reflect on your FIST Factor and make sure no nay-sayers have infiltrated your mental space and are diverting your trajectory toward Point B and off of Point C.

7. Sign up and expose yourself to fast-hit social media outlets and deliverables that are in alignment with your TC.

# About the Author

Dr. Jeffrey Magee, PDM, CSP, CMC, has been called one of today's "leading leadership and marketing strategists." Jeff is the author of more than 20 books, two college textbooks, and four best-sellers, and is the publisher of *PERFORMANCE/P360 Magazine* (www.ProfessionalPerformanceMagazine.com). He is also the former cohost of the national business entrepreneur program on Catalyst Business Radio (www.catalystbusinessradio.com/index .php), and Human Capital Developer for more than 20 years with www.JeffreyMagee.com.

Raised on a farm, Jeff started his first business at age 15 and sold it before going to college. By age 24, he was recognized by American Home Products, a Fortune 500 company, as its top salesman in the nation, while at the same time becoming the youngest certified sales instructor for the Dale Carnegie Sales Course. After experiencing downsizing in 1987, he went on to work as a sales associate for the nation's largest educational and youth advertising/marketing firm, Target Marketing, and was promoted to vice president of sales and chief operating officer within two years.

Jeff's credentials are significant. He is a Certified Speaking Professional, a Certified Management Consultant, and a Certified Professional Direct Marketer. He has been recognized as one of the "Ten Outstanding Young Americans" (TOYA) by the U.S. Junior Chamber of Commerce, and was twice selected to represent the United States at the World Congress as a Leadership Speaker (Cannes, France and Vienna, Austria). A three-term president of the Oklahoma Speakers Association and twice honored with their Professional Speaker Member of the Year award, today, the Chapter's outstanding member of the year is awarded the "Jeff Magee Member of the Year Award." Jeff served for four years as an appointed Civil Service Commissioner (Judge) for the City/County of Tulsa, Oklahoma, before relocating to Montana.

Today, Jeff is the author of the nationally syndicated "Leadership" column that you may have seen in your local business newspaper. He is the author of more than 20 leadership, performance, and sales books that have been transcribed into multiple languages. His text, *Yield Management* (also known as *The Managerial-Leadership Bible*) has been a number-one-selling graduate management school textbook, while *The Sales Training Handbook* (McGraw-Hill) was an instant best-seller and has been transcribed into more than 20 languages.

Many of the Fortune 100 firms today use Jeff for Performance Execution® in the areas of managerial-leadership effectiveness, human capital performance, and sales training and coaching. He also been invited as a keynote speaker at many major associations in the United States, and to speak at West Point Military Academy on leadership.

Jeff was commissioned to design, train, and present a new series of national leadership and sales recruitment programs for the more than 5,000 professional sales recruiters and sales managers with the U.S. Army National Guard. For this, he has subsequently received the prestigious Commander's Coin of Excellence.

In 2010, while merging his business of 20 years, Jeff Magee International (Tulsa, Oklahoma), with WesternCPE (Bozeman, Montana), he was recognized by the U.S. Small Business Commerce Association's (SBCA) 2010 Best of Business Award in the lecture bureau category. The SBCA Best of Business Award Program recognizes the best small businesses throughout the country. Using consumer feedback and other research, the SBCA identifies companies that they believe have demonstrated what makes small businesses a vital part of the American economy. The selection committee chooses the award winners from nominees based on information taken from monthly surveys administered by the SBCA, a review of consumer rankings, and other consumer reports. Award winners are a valuable asset to their community and exemplify what makes small businesses great.

In 2011 Jeff unmerged from WesternCPE to continue with his own firm, JeffreyMagee.com (Leadership Training & Technology/What You Need To Succeed!), and has been a regular content provider to AICPA, WesternCPE, Boomer Consulting, iShade, CPELink, and many Fortune 500 firms and government agencies, as well as appearing regularly at major conventions and conferences around the world. Jeff is known to many as the thought leaders' thought leader!

The *London Business Gazette* has hailed Jeff as "An American Business Guru." Former President George W. Bush and the U.S. Army National Guard recognized him with the high honor of the "Total Team Victory & Freedom Award."

*To book Jeff*: Jeff can be scheduled for your next conference, convention, or retreat, or for consulting or an onsite high-impact, results-driven development program, by contacting DrJeffSpeaks@aol.com.

# Index

**A**

A letter, attitude, 64
Accelerated ROI, 145
Accountability, immediate, 154
Accountability mechanisms, 93
Action plans, 112
    feedback with, 97
Airlines, 44
A-level people, 27, 75
Alice in Wonderland (Carroll, L.),
        25
Alignment of trajectory, 145
American Express, 53
American Institute of Certified
        Accountants (AICPA), 60
Anheuser-Busch, 43
Armstrong, Lance, 82
Assertiveness, 166
Association for Talent Department
        (ATD), 94
Athletes, 53
    metaphor, 50
    professionals, 73

**B**

Bad credit, 140
Badger, Graeme, 87
Behavior(s), 30
    change in, 95
    outward, 81
    passive-aggressive, 122
Belief vs. right and. wrong, 102
Benchmark, 25
Blending, attempted, 148
Blessings in disguise, 96
B-level people, 27, 75
Boeing, 43
Bosses, 100
Brain:
    conscious, 82
    model, 82

performance, 81
    regions, 83
Branson, Richard, 82
Bridge deployment, 109
Buffett, Warren, 82

**C**

C letter:
    capability, 62
    culture, 66
    understanding of, 67
C route, of trajectory, 109
Calibration, and recalibration, 117
Capabilities:
    level of, 68
    overall, 65
Categories, importance of, 86
CEOs, 43, 60
Certified public accountants, (CPAs), 69
Change agents, 122
Cheshire Cat, 25
Childhood, 14, 86, 93–94
Circle, physical or mental, 18
C-level people, 27
Coaching for Impact (Magee, J. and
        Kent-Ferraro, J.), 25
College mission statement, 32
Collegiate varsity athletes, 50
Comments, behavior specific, 65
Commitment, 95
Communication, 166
Communication engagement model, 25
Community, 84
Competence, 55
Competency capital, 60
Complacency, 74
The Conference Board, 60
Constituents, 129
Constructive dialogues, internal, 17
Conversations, internal and external, 59
Core beliefs. *See* Trajectory Code imprint

Core capabilities, 62
Core competencies. *See* Trajectory Code
    imprint
Core Driver, 167
Cornerstone variables, 166
CPA X-Factor, 69
Cross learn, 97
Cultural imprints, 66
Culture:
  benefits of, 66–67
  as calibrator, 112
  second guessing, 111–112
  smart meaning of, 123
  Southwest Airlines, 44
Customer mission statement, 32

**D**

Defeats and successes, inventory of,
    17
Deposits, 140
Destiny:
  immediate, 159
  intermediate, 159
  long-term, 159
Dialogue(s):
  inner, 19
  negative, 60
  negative vs. constructive, 17
Discipline, breakdown in, 94
DNA:
  development, 68
  of group, 68
  human capital DNA, 66, 72
  mental childhood DNA, 41
  mental DNA, 62
  mental TC DNA imprint, 14
  performance execution DNA,
    86
DNA variables, 68
Douglas, Gabby, 16
Dress, 98

**E**

E letter:
  expectations, 67
  experiences, 65
  understanding of, 67
E2, expectations, 67

Education, 84
  for jobs, 112
Efforts, concentration of, 41
80 = followers, 116
Emotional Quotient (EQ), 61, 72, 75
Emotions, 83
Endeavors, human capital, 73
End-points, 129, 132
Energies, windshield or rear-view, 19
Enough Already (Magee, J.), 103
Entrepreneurial leadership, 96
EQ (Emotional Quotient), 61, 72, 75
  factors, 69
Execution, future, 59
Expectations:
  E letter, 67
  E2, 67
  high, 153
  low, 153
  of others, 85
  self-expectations, 61
  trajectory, 42

**F**

Family, 19
Family aspects, 84
Favoritism, 145
Feedback, behavior based, 64
Financial stability, 84
FIST Factor™:
  applying to, 81
  being fed, 82
  changes for, 95
  concept, 87
  destructive, 137
  dialog from, 89
  direct imprint upon, 111
  effects of, 85
  influencers, 84
  internal teeter-totter, 81
  knowledge about, 103
  lack of, 111
  members of, 114
  model, 89
  model as a tool, 113
  references, 117
  retooling, 148
  review of, 137

situation, 86
smart meaning of, 123
strategic members of, 93
understandable, 104
unhealthy, 102, 145
5W and 1H model, 28
Followers vs. transformers, 121
Forces, trajectory-shaping, 94
Forecasting, 99
Formula, diagnostic, 62–63
Friend, 19
Fundamental commonality, as objective
        diagnostic, 59
Future:
    altering, 159
    execution, 59
    vs. forecast, 26
    performance, 59
    trajectory, 28, 137

**G**

Gap:
    address, 113
    bridging, 112, 114–115, 117, 166
    development, 110
    knowledge, 113
    between Point B and Point C, 109, 112
Gaps-n-Cracks, 98
GE, 43
Generation, education, 112
Gerstner, Louis, 53, 74
GIGO (garbage in, garbage out), 18
GPS idea, 167
Growth, 166
Guilt by association, 130

**H**

Habits, 83, 111
Harley-Davidson, 70
Health and fitness, 84
High expectations, trajectory of, 153
High maintenance appearance, 131
Human capital:
    development, 61
    development plan, 73
    DNA, 66, 72
    endeavors, 73
    inventory of, 72

lack of talent, 122
performance, 60
pool, 110
strategic plan, 60
X-Factor, 61

**I**

Identity factor, 26
Identity-Purpose (IP) Statement:
    baseline, 113
    decaying, 137
    defining, 31
    demonstration of, 104
    effects of, 30, 85
    evaluating, 49
    example of, 28
    and FIST Factor™, 30
    influence of, 27
    influence on Trajectory Code, 33
    lack of depth, 60
    others without, 83
    outdated, 145
    Player Capability Index (PCI) and, 45
    questions about, 30
    retooling, 148
    revealing, 132
    smart meaning of, 123
    studying, 117
    and Trajectory Code, 33
    understanding the implications, 25–27
Immelt, Jeff, 43
Implosion, 67, 121, 138
Imprinting, 14–16, 160
Imprints:
    introducing new, 161
    phantom, 20
    positive, 13
    receipt of, 54
    on Trajectory Code, 13
    of your life, 55
Individuals:
    negative, 83
    vs. transformers, 83
Influencers:
    balanced teeter-tot, 85
    life-balanced, 84
    positive personal, 81
    types of, 19, 88

Influences, teeter-totter, 86
Information Grams, 99–100
Inspiration, 84
Intelligence Quotient (IQ), 61, 72, 75
Internal conversations, 13
Intervention, 95
Investment, in yourself, 100
IQ (Intelligence Quotient), 61, 69, 72, 75

**J**

Job responsibilities, 97
Juice and success, 53

**K**

K-Factor space, 168
Knowledge, acquisition, 64
Knowledge edge, 113

**L**

Ladder metaphor, 18
Lateral trajectory, 129
Leadership development team, 43
Legacy, 28, 147
LINE, 59, 81, 87, 94, 98, 168
Line's direction, 19
Listening, to self-talk, 161
London Olympics, 54
Low expectations, 153

**M**

Master Mind, 93
Memories, 83
Mental Action Plan (MAP), 33
Mental childhood DNA, 41
Mental DNA, 62
Mental drivers, internal, 88
Mental imprints, of Trajectory Code, 121
Mental space, 17
Mental TC DNA imprint, 14
Mentor, 72
Mirror effectively, 98
Motivation:
  establishing programs, 39
  Southwest Airlines, 44
  variable, 166

**N**

Negative dialogues, 17
Negativity, 13
Neocortex, 81
Nepotism, smart meaning of, 123
Networking and personal tagline, 97

**O**

O = Organize Options, 114
1 percent calibration, 109
1 percent factors, 98, 104, 145, 149, 154
Opportunities, identification, 41
Organization mission statement, 31
Organizational Growth, 21, 34, 46, 56, 78, 90, 105, 118, 124, 133, 141–142, 150, 154, 162
Origin, 13
Others:
  blending with, 145–146
  depth of, 130
  interactions or relationships, 137
  management by, 132
  Player Capability Index™ (PCI) depth, 132
  Point C of, 147
  value line within PFC FISHES™, 132
Overdraft protection, 140
Ownership:
  assuming, 42
  assumption of, 44
  competency, 43
  issues, 40
  level of, 39
  as by-product, 40

**P**

P = Pick and Proceed, 114
P letter:
  accounting environment, 69
  as guideposts, 73
  performance, 64
  understanding of, 67
Pain, 148
Pain factor, 147
Pain points, 122
Passion, faked, 42
Pathway B, 159

Pathway C, 159
PCI formula, 75
Peer Accountability, 72
Peer group, 130
Peer-to-Peer Influence Accountability, 46,
    55–56, 78, 90, 105, 118,
    124–125, 133, 141, 149, 154
Peer-to-peer interactions, 45, 166
People:
    challenging and different, 102
    limiting exposure to difficult, 103
    windshield vs. review-mirror, 15
Performance:
    execution resistance, 83
    future, 59
    review systems, 54
Performance execution:
    application, 43
    brain model, 82
    DNA, 86
    effectiveness, 60, 67
    ensuing, 44
    excellence, 64, 67
    future, 59
    greatness, 53
    at highest level, 83
    lack of, 82
    level of, 74, 81, 89
    meaningful outcome future, 40
    as net result, 75
    outcomes, 61
    possibilities, 87
    search for, 70
    sources of, 52
    stature, 87
    success, 49, 83, 86
    and trajectory achievement, 71
Performance Quotient (PQ), 69, 72,
    75
Performance review, 65
Performance review instrument, 73
Performance success, 42
Performance trajectory, 65
Personal (Positional) Growth, 21, 34,
    45–46, 55, 78, 89–90,
    104–105, 118, 124–125, 133,
    141, 149, 154, 162
Personal development time, 168
Personal habits, 110–111

Personal mission statement, 32
Personal trajectory growth, 45, 166
PFC FISHES™, 166
    applying to life trajectory, 81–90
    categories, 86, 88
    goals within, 86
    Life-Balance diagram, 86
    model, 84, 87, 89
    model reference, 97
    others value line within, 132
    value line within, 130
Phantom imprints, 20
Phelps, Michael, 54, 82
Pig farm, 86
Plant Capability Index, 113
Player Capability Index™ (PCI):
    abilities, 77
    application of, 145, 153
    calibration, 14, 159
    calibrators, 28, 59, 112
    category within, 100
    culture factors, 66
    depth of, 87, 98
    design of, 28
    development, 75
    diagram, 159
    enhancer time, 168
    findings, 72
    and FIST Factor™, 17
    for foresight, 99
    formula, 71, 77
    growth, 83
    Identity-Purpose Statement influence
      on, 33
    implications of, 25
    imprint influence on, 14
    imprints, 13, 167
    independent, 121
    influence on, 27
    maintaining, 109
    model, 61, 70, 74, 168
    positive, 18
    references, 117
    reinforced, 45
    relationships, 68
    smart meaning of, 123
    strengths, 146–147
    strengths from, 161
    strengths shown, 97

Player Capability Index™ (*continued*)
  sum of, 29
  understanding, 95
Pleasure factor, 147
Point A, 25, 27, 167
  trajectory calibration at, 103
Point B:
  disappointment, 67
  GPS concept, 167
  pathway, 95
  to Point C, 89, 96
  trajectories, 54, 67
  trajectory away from, 103
  trajectory pathway to, 31
  trajectory towards, 30
Point B and Point C, 113–114
Point C:
  for always-intended goals, 27, 167
  attachment, 14
  demand for, 110
  by design, 53
  destinations, 103
  endings, 166
  engagement for success, 161
  experiences, 53
  long-term, 138
  of others, 147
  Point B to, 96
  rewards from, 89
  success, 161
  targets, 33
  trajectory from, 110
  trajectory pathway to, 31
  trajectory pathways, 130
  trajectory towards, 33
Point C destinations:
  appearances of, 60
  balanced, 19, 64
  calibration influencers, 54
  calibrators, 19, 59, 67, 70
  contributors, 16
  enrichment, 65
  and Identity-Purpose Statement, 30
  influence of, 61
  influencers, 53
  influences, 20
  make-up, 16
  members of, 27, 76

  multiple, 17
  positive influences, 161
  reinforcement, 45
  shaping, 49
  situational-driven, 17
  and Trajectory Code, 17
  trajectory of, 25, 45
Policy cycle, strategic plan, 60
Positive imprints, 13
Posture, 81
Posturing, defensive, 122
PQ (Performance Quotient), 69, 72, 75
Presenters, trapped, 101
Presenter's Box, 101
Primal behaviors, 159
Profession, 19
Professional aspects, 84
Professional feedback, 54
Professional organization, ownership of, 45
Professionals, surveys of, 60
Proficiency, 96
Psychology, for changes, 95
Purpose factor, 26

**Q**

Questions:
  behind questions, 160
  responses to, 86

**R**

R letter:
  relationships, 68
  results, 62, 68–69
Reading, 168
Realignment, trajectory recalibrator, 113
Reality, 27
Real-time assessment, 53
Rearview-mirror:
  disappointments, 50
  flashing back, 74
  images, 13
Recalibrations, 52, 104
  opportunities from, 109
Re-Do You, 20, 45, 77–78, 89–90, 104–105, 117–118, 124–125, 132–133, 141–142, 149–150, 154–155

Relationship Cube™, 138–140, 166
Relationships:
    applications of, 68
    architecture of, 138
    natural lifecycle, 140
    situational, 137
    strength of, 139
Reputation, 131
Responsibilities:
    accountable for, 103
    clarification, 103
    influencers, 87
    of jobs, 97
    ownership of, 39
    succession development transition of,
        61
Return of investment (ROI), accelerated,
    145
Rhetoric, 110
Right and wrong vs. belief, 102
RJR Nabisco, 53
ROI (return on investment), 109
Rule 80–10–10, 114–115

**S**

S = Start the process over, 114
S = Stop and See, 114
Safe decisions:
    reasons for, 121
    vs. smart decisions, 121, 123
Scholarships, 50
School, academic problems in, 94
Schweitzer, Brian, 76–77
Self accountability and structure, 94
Self-esteem, 39, 41–42
Self-expectations, influence of, 61
Self-reflecting, 63
Self-talk:
    about questions, 75
    impacts to, 83
    listening to, 161
    negative, 18, 73
Shift drivers:
    chronological psychological order,
        95
    encountering, 96
    recognition of, 166
    trajectory, 93

    trajectory calibration, 103
    trajectory generation, 101
Shift happens, 93–105
Skills, 99
Smart, meanings of, 123
Social circle, 84
Social media, 68–69
Society for Human Resource
        Management (SHRM), 94
Solutions, plural, 102
Southwest Airlines, 44, 70
Spiritual, 85
Standard operating procedure (SOP), 111
Stanford University, 82
Starting point, 40
Stature, 87
STOPS™ model:
    gap assessment, 113
    letters meaning, 114
    smart meaning of, 123
    transformers participation, 116
Strategies, effective, 93
"Suc" factor, 71, 74–75, 83
"Suc" zone, 52–53
Success:
    by association, 130
    defining, 20
    performance execution, 49
    road to, 53
    vs. "suc," 51
    and victories, 40
Success factor, 51, 75
Success quotient, 86
Surveys, real-time electronic, 60

**T**

T = Target and Think, 114
T letter:
    formal education, 69
    as guideposts, 73
    vs. A letter, 70
    two interpretations of, 63
    understanding of, 67
Tactics, to trajectory success, 93
Tax advice, 69
TC:
    calibration, 81
    collective, 81

TC (*continued*)
  direct imprint upon, 111
  makeover, 88
  understanding of, 27
TC development, 65
TC direction calibrators, 16
TC enrichment, 65
TC ideas, 71
TC ideologies, 99
Team mission statement, 31–32
Teams, integration in, 99
Technical skill sets, 63
Teeter-totter:
  influencers comparison to, 84
  mental, 83
  retooling, 148
  and TC, 88
Teeter-totter metaphor, 81, 83
Teeter-totter variables, 83
10 = influencer groups enlistable, 116
10 = influencer groups to change, 116
Them, 110
Thought capacity, independent, 121
Time, 111
Tough love, 53
Training, training, 63
Trajectory:
  abandoning, 148
  achievement and performance
      execution, 71
  alignment of, 145
  blending, 131, 145
  calibration clue, 81
  chance interaction, 137
  changes, 68, 95
  collision points, 129
  destructive, 85
  entrepreneurial success, 93
  experiences and end-points, 129
  future, 28, 137
  of high expectations, 153
  implications of, 166
  lateral, 129
  of long-term points, 130
  misfires, 109
  ramifications, 93
  recalibration, 166
  self-destructive, 145
  shifts, 93

  of smart decision, 121
  smart meaning of, 123
  ultimate acceleration, 137, 140
  variables affecting, 101
Trajectory "C," members of, 76
Trajectory calibration, 147
  diagram, 27
Trajectory Code, 50
  calibration, 54
  imprint, 160–161
  imprints, 94
  influencers, 53
  mental imprints of, 121
  for peak performance, 54
  pushed forward, 53
  shaping, 94, 153
Trajectory Code (TC), constructive, 104
Trajectory course C, 112
Trajectory course variable, 16
Trajectory derailers, 140
Trajectory destinations, 161
Trajectory direction, 27
  level of, 17
  successes and achievements, 44
  work through, 49
Trajectory expectation, 42
Trajectory experiences, 129
Trajectory imprints, 65
Trajectory pathways, 51–52, 130, 146,
      161, 166–167
Trajectory point, 93
Trajectory success, 41, 44, 53
Trajectory track C, 167
Transformers:
  vs. followers, 121
  vs. individuals, 83
  references as valuable and loyal, 116
  support of, 147
Trust, 166

**U**

Under-dog, 20
Unique Selling Feature, 101
Us, 110

**V**

Value accountability, 111
Value calibrators, 139

Values. *See* Trajectory Code imprint
Variables, cornerstone, 166
Vertical trajectory, 131
Victories:
    establishing, 39
    lackluster, 42
    mid-level, 54
    and success, 40
    vs. victimhood, 159
Victors vs. victims, 44
VIPs, 75
Voices, limited, 18
Volunteer activities, 97–98

**W**

Weaknesses, 41–42
Wedge categories, 86
Welch, Jack, 43
"What" factor, 26
WIIFM (what's in it for me), 146
WIIFU (what's in it for us), 146
William of Ockham, 93
Windshield:
    dialogue and conversations, 59
    emotional, 159
    forward time, 17
    language, 54
    perspectives, 18
    "success," 50
    TC direction calibrators, 16
Windshield or rear-view mirror:
    behavior, 26
    future forecast vs. forecast, 26

    vs. rear-mirror operations, 111
    situation doubts, 31
Winfrey, Oprah, 82
Woods, Tiger, 82
Word choice, 81
Work, through meaningful trajectory, 49
Work ethic, 94, 111
Workplace, residence in, 60

**X**

X (endeavor), 49
X-Factor:
    answers to, 69
    development, 75
    development plan, 73
    domain, 69
    dominance, 71
    grasp on, 49
    identify, 59
    life changing model, 51
    opportunities from, 87
    in plans, 54
    revelation about, 59
    tendencies, 84
    X representation in, 49

**Y**

You, 109–110

**Z**

Ziglar, Zig, 146